The Earls &

of

Devonshire

by
Julie Bunting

ISBN 0 946404 25 9

1998

The Derbyshire Heritage Series

Happy Walking International Ltd.,
Unit 1, Molyneux Business Park,
Whitworth Road,
Darley Dale, Matlock,
Derbyshire.
DE4 2HJ

Happy Walking International Ltd.,
Unit 1,
Molyneux Business Park,
Whitworth Road,
Darley Dale,
Matlock,
Derbyshire
DE4 2HJ
Tel/Fax 01629 - 735911

Printed, bound, marketed and distributed by Happy Walking International Ltd.

© Text - Julie Bunting 1996.

First Published - August 1996.
This reprint - August 1997.

ISBN 1 874754 70 5

British Library Cataloguing-in-Publication Data. A catalogue record of this book is available from the British Library.

Typset in Times - bold, italic, and plain 10pt, 14pt and 18pt.

Cover © Happy Walking Ltd.

Contents

Page No.

Introduction by His Grace the Duke of Devonshire.................................4

Introductory Notes 5

The First Earl of Devonshire - 1552-1625 6

The Second Earl of Devonshire - 1590 - 1628 9

The Third Earl of Devonshire - 1617 - 1684 12

The Fourth Earl of Devonshire - Part 1 - 1640 - 1694 15

The First Duke of Devonshire - Part 11 - 1694 - 1707 19

The Second Duke of Devonshire - 1673 - 1729 22

The Third Duke of Devonshire - 1698 - 1755 25

The Fourth Duke of Devonshire - 1720 - 1764 28

The Fifth Duke of Devonshire - 1748 - 1811 31

The Sixth Duke of Devonshire - 1790 - 1858 35

The Seventh Duke of Devonshire - 1808 - 1891 39

The Eighth Duke of Devonshire - 1833 - 1908 42

The Ninth Duke of Devonshire - 1868 - 1938 46

The Tenth Duke of Devonshire - 1895 - 1950 50

The Eleventh Duke of Devonshire 54

Family Tree 62

The Derbyshire Heritage Series....................................63

INTRODUCTION BY HIS GRACE
THE DUKE OF DEVONSHIRE

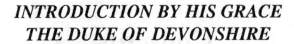

These biographies of my predecessors initially appeared in the Peak Advertiser in 1994 to commemorate the tercentenary of the creation of the Devonshire Dukedom.

It was already clear from comments made by many of the tens of thousands of annual visitors to Chatsworth that there is wide interest in the lives of those earlier generations who have left their mark here. People are often surprised to learn that the majority of these Earls and Dukes of Devonshire also played much wider roles, extending to both British and international affairs. They earned the confidence of Kings and Queens, the respect of politicians and the trust of people from all walks of life.

Each successor to the title has displayed distinct attributes of his own, yet they have shared an extraordinary tenacity in keeping Chatsworth intact - aided, it must be said, by primogeniture. But for this oft-criticised feudal rule whereby the eldest son is sole heir to his father's estate, Chatsworth and its contents would have been split up long ago.

In fact my ancestors and I have been remarkably fortunate both in marrying well and in fathering sons to continue the line. Wives, mistresses and widows have influenced Cavendish history too, indeed the whole story began with a most formidable woman who lived in the Elizabethan England of more than four centuries ago, Bess of Hardwick.

The beginning, then is clear. With optimism for the future I am content that this ongoing story is left without an end.

Chatsworth, April 1995

Chatsworth Old Hall.

THE EARLS AND DUKES OF DEVONSHIRE
(Introductory notes:)

The Devonshire title has now been handed down through fourteen generations of the House of Cavendish, firstly to Earls and then to Dukes.

The shrewd talents of their ancestress, Bess of Hardwick, are an equally important part of their inheritance and have often been called upon in full measure, especially in recent, literally taxing, times.

For more than four centuries, Cavendishes have remained close to national events, the Devonshire dukedom being one of their early rewards. In private they have awarded themselves rather more passing pleasures: gambling, drinking, collecting, spending - and love. Their paramours, countesses and duchesses have themselves shaped the course of events on occasion, sharing in scandals and schemings, financial turbulence and, ultimately, rescue.

Such stories are revealed behind these portraits of men of their times, a few of whom have squandered much of their once massive birthright but the majority intent on keeping it secure for the future. It is that streak of determination which has saved their magnificent family seat, Chatsworth, to become one of the nation's greatest treasures.

5

Monument to Henry and William Cavendish, Edensor Church.

THE FIRST EARL OF DEVONSHIRE (1552 - 1625)

Why the first Earl adopted the county of Devon for his title could never be accounted for. William Cavendish was not in fact born to inherit the vast wealth which would bring him the title of Earl although it was fortunate for future generations that events unfolded as they did.

6

William was the second son of Sir William Cavendish and Bess of Hardwick. Bess's first husband, Robert Barlow, already 'sick of the Chronical Distemper' at the time of their teenage marriage, left her a childless widow whilst still very young and Bess was aged only about twenty when she married the twice-widowed Sir William Cavendish in 1547

Sir William had earlier been well rewarded by Henry VIII for his role in securing monastic properties at the dissolution, not only being given a knighthood and the position of Treasurer of the King's chamber, but generous grants of former monastic land. He was to continue to receive royal favour - and more landed property - from Edward VI, retaining his office under both Edward and then Mary Tudor.

This wealth was all to be converted into Derbyshire property during his marriage to Bess, beginning with the purchase of the manor house of Chatsworth in 1549 for £600. The property was put into their joint names. Bess's ambitions to replace it with a magnificent new Chatsworth House ultimately left her husband in the serious position of having to explain to Queen Mary why £5,000 was missing from the accounts of the royal chamber. In the event Bess herself was left with the problem when Sir William died in 1557 with the debt still unsettled. It was only her personal friendship with Elizabeth I which eventually enabled her to settle the matter, at a greatly reduced figure, without having to sell her beloved Chatsworth.

AFFECTION AND ACRIMONY

Meanwhile, this most eligible widow had quickly contracted another favourable, albeit affectionate, match. Her third husband was the wealthy Sir William St. Loe. Bess brought six young Cavendish children to the marriage, all treated admirably by their otherwise childless step-father who also paid for the two oldest boys, Henry and William, to attend Eton. St. Loe died in 1564 but three years later his step-children's future was assured beyond question when their mother took for her fourth husband George Talbot, Sixth Earl of Shrewsbury.

This marriage ended in acrimony, yet when the Countess of Shrewsbury was widowed for the last time in 1590 she managed to keep the Shrewsbury wealth, making her the richest woman in England after the Queen. Bess was determined to settle the bulk of these assets on her son, William Cavendish. William has often been written of as her favourite son but the fact is that his older brother, Henry, was such an unworthy heir that he and Bess had been estranged long before she died in 1608. Fortunately for the 'succession' Henry fathered only illegitimate children; his activities as 'the common bull of Derbyshire and Staffordshire' were common knowledge.

It was due to his large debts that Henry had to sell Chatsworth, with its valuable income from rents, to William. At least, too, Henry died in good time for his younger brother to take the family's vast fortune into his capable care.

AN EARLDOM

William Cavendish was by now in his mid-sixties and married to his second wife, Elizabeth, by whom he had a son. His first wife, Anne, had borne him three sons and three daughters but of the former only his namesake, William, survived him.

The first family had lived at Hardwick during the later part of Bess's life but whilst William was by nature a modest and rather frugal man, deeply committed to his interests in Derbyshire, there were benefits to be gained from his social standing, his wealth, and not least his keen business acumen. Careful not to chance his inheritance he invested in foreign trading companies, reinvesting his profits wisely.

Shortly before he reached the age of thirty William received a knighthood from Elizabeth I. Under James I, on the occasion of the christening of the Princess Sophia in May 1605, he was created Baron Cavendish of Hardwicke. In the intervening years he had acted as MP for Liverpool and for Newport, served as High Sheriff of Derbyshire, and was later appointed Knight of the Bath.

William, Lord Cavendish, was to receive something even more important to bequeath to his heirs - an earldom. On 2 August 1618 he was created Earl of Devonshire during a stay at the Bishop of Salisbury's palace with the King and his court, though the honour reputedly cost him £10,000. The following year he was named Lord Lieutenant of Derbyshire, official representative of the Crown with responsibility for the judiciary and militia in his home county.

Through all of these roles his first duties, as ever, were to his birthright and at his death, on 3 March 1625, a very healthy inheritance awaited his son and heir, another William Cavendish.

Thomas Hobbes.

THE SECOND EARL OF DEVONSHIRE
(1590 - 1628)

William Cavendish, oldest surviving son and namesake of the First Earl of Devonshire, was cast in a very different mould to his cautious and frugal father. But the younger William was also the first-born grandson of Bess of Hardwick and therein lay a clue to his self-willed, even self-indulgent, character.

The Cavendish matriarch was closely concerned with the upbringing of this future heir to her estates and was a figure of undoubted influence during her remaining lifetime, the first eighteen years of William's life.

Yet, just as Bess had found her authority challenged by her oldest son, Henry, so her second son William - to whom the estates eventually passed - met with a similar problem. It was on the question of marriage that the young William, almost out of his teens now, rebelled. With his inheritance, gilded by a knighthood received two years earlier, he could not have expected a love match nor even much of a say in his choice of bride. Certainly the regularisation of his liaison with a lady of his grandmother's household, some years his senior, was out of the question.

The tender years of his prospective bride gave the youth extra cause to stand up to his father, for Christian Bruce was only twelve years old. William even held his ground when King James strongly backed this wealthy match as a returned favour to the girl's father, Lord Kinloss. The King personally contributed to her £10,000 dowry .

Eventually young Sir William capitulated: it was essential for an aspiring courtier to retain royal favour. Furthermore a blind eye towards his mistress was promised whilst his child-bride grew up. In practice the groom was free to pursue the pleasures of Court to the full. Historian John Pearson in *Stags and Serpents* describes him as 'the contemporary ideal of a presentable young aristocrat', equipped with all the social graces acquired through an expensive education, coupled with a chivalrous, dashing air and an eye for fashion.

THE LINGUIST & THE PHILOSOPHER

Aimless as this lifestyle was - and Cavendish, furthermore, lived in reckless extravagance - it did have the singular advantage of introducing him to far wider schools of thought than he would have encountered outside the capital. He had the good fortune to make a close friend for life of Thomas Hobbes. An Oxford graduate and classics scholar, Hobbes was only a couple of years the elder yet found in Cavendish a keen pupil in philosophical matters. In 1610 the two young men toured France, Germany and Italy, an invaluable experience for them both. The dandy came home an accomplished linguist and the scholar returned to prepare to make his mark as a philosopher.

In 1618 when his father was created Earl of Devonshire, the younger William became Lord Cavendish. The following year, jointly with his father, he served as Lord Lieutenant of Derbyshire, having already completed his first spell as MP for the county. His first son, another William, had been born in 1617, to be followed three years later by a brother, Charles.

By now Governor of the Bermudas Company, Cavendish enjoyed a large income. He was assisted in financial matters by his friend Hobbes in the role of secretary. In 1623 differing interests within the Company brought two factions into dispute; Cavendish stood at the head of one, the Earl of Warwick at the other. A heated argument between the two men took them to the brink of a duel and resulted in Cavendish being reprimanded for issuing intense personal insults against the Earl.

DEBT & DAMAGE

Lord Cavendish lived in splendid style, with expense no object, in Bishopsgate. He continued to be a leading figure at Court after Charles I came to the throne and was a guest at the King's marriage to Henrietta Maria in 1625. Upon the death of the First Earl of Devonshire the following year, Cavendish inherited the title and a seat in the House of Lords.

For some years he had maintained a lavish lifestyle only by borrowing against his future inheritance. With this wealth released into his profligate hands, it was soon apparent that he had severely drained even the ample Cavendish resources. In the year after his father's death the new Earl was forced to introduce a bill in the House of Lords to enable him to sell land from his entailed estates.

More personal damage was beyond redemption; in June of the following year, 1628, the Second Earl of Devonshire died at Bishopsgate 'of excessive indulgence in good living'. His body was brought back to Derby All Saints Church, now the Cathedral, for burial.

The widowed Countess Christian was left with enormous debts and nearly thirty lawsuits. Yet, demonstrating a Scottish shrewdness and a gift for financial budgeting, she devoted herself to protecting her children's inheritance - the Third Earl was aged only eleven when his father died. Severe economies pruned the servants, disposed of some land and ended all social spending, Even Thomas Hobbes was suspended. When finances permitted he was reinstated as tutor to the young Earl, who at the age of twenty-one took over Chatsworth House and the wealth once so closely threatened by his late father.

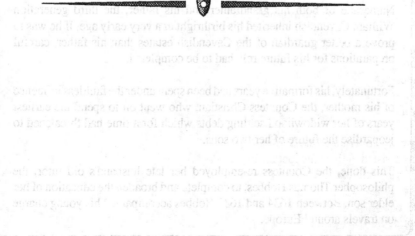

The old church at Peak Forest.

THE THIRD EARL OF DEVONSHIRE
(1617 - 1684)

Namesake of both his grandfather and his father, the third generation William Cavendish inherited his birthright at a very early age. If he was to prove a better guardian of the Cavendish estates than his father, careful preparations for his future role had to be completed.

Fortunately, his formative years had been spent under the faultless influence of his mother, the Countess Christian, who went on to spend the earliest years of her widowhood settling debts which for a time had threatened to jeopardise the future of her two sons.

This done, the Countess re-employed her late husband's old tutor, the philosopher Thomas Hobbes, to complete and broaden the education of her elder son. Between 1634 and 1637 Hobbes accompanied his young charge on travels around Europe.

In 1639 the handsome Third Earl of Devonshire married Elizabeth Cecil, daughter of the Second Earl of Shrewsbury. The previous year he had completed his first term of office as Lord Lieutenant of Derbyshire, following which he became High Steward of Ampthill and joint Commissioner of Array for Leicestershire.

The Cavendishes continued in royal favour. As a child, William had been created Knight of the Bath at the coronation of Charles I, and the Countess Christian became a trusted friend of Queen Henrietta Maria. It was inevitable that this prominent Royalist family became drawn into the Civil War when it came. From the start the Earl and his younger brother, Charles, put their fortunes and their lives at the disposal of the King. Charles Cavendish, the epitome of a brave and gallant cavalier, raised a regiment at his own expense and saw repeated action as its bold colonel. He rode close behind Prince Rupert in the cavalry charge at Edgehill and distinguished himself sufficiently to be given command of Royalist forces in Lincolnshire and Nottinghamshire. At the age of twenty-three he fell on the field when his soldiers faced Cromwell at Gainsborough in 1643.

It was in memory of Charles Cavendish that his mother built the chapel at Peak Forest. Only after Restoration of the Monarchy was it dedicated to St. Charles, King and Martyr, according to her wishes.

William, meanwhile, had been present with King Charles at York in 1642, in which year he was expelled from the House of Lords and ordered to stand committed to the Tower. This followed his refusal to take his place in parliament, for which he was impeached together with eight other peers of high crimes and misdemeanours.

Well aware of the potential dangers of political protest, the Earl left England to live in France, upon which his estates were sequestrated. The Dowager Countess watched events with dismay. The death of her younger son made William's survival paramount and she used her still-strong influence to persuade him to return to England and, of vital importance, to appear willing to compromise his Royalist sympathies by submitting to parliament.

The Earl was pardoned upon a fine of £5,000 and went to live with his mother in her Buckinghamshire home, Latimers. There King Charles spent one night as their guest in the middle of October 1645. After a time the Earl did move back to his childhood home, Hardwick Hall, but had to wait for the Restoration before he could return to Chatsworth, which had been occupied by both sides in turn during the Civil War.

UPKEEP AND UPDATING

The unassuming lifestyle of the Third Earl, coupled with the disturbances of recent years, left him with no inclination to squander his inheritance. During the Common-wealth he had been restricted to acting as its guardian but once back at Chatsworth he was able to set about attending to its upkeep and restoring order. Updating the great

13

house revealed the first worrying indications of major faults in its proportions when cracks opened up in the masonry.

In 1660 the Earl was reappointed Lord Lieutenant of Derbyshire and Steward of Tutbury before becoming Steward of the High Peak. Having, literally, put his house in order he allowed himself more time to study literature and science. He started to assemble a library which has since grown into perhaps the most important and valuable in private hands in England. Much credit for its foundation must go to his lifelong companion Thomas Hobbes, by this time famous throughout Europe as author of *Leviathan*. This work was much despised but the philosopher remained under the family's devoted wing until he ended his days in their household in 1679.

William Cavendish survived old Thomas Hobbes by only five years. He died on 23 November 1684 at his house at Roehampton but was laid to rest at Edensor. His widow Elizabeth survived him by five years. Their son and only surviving child, another William, succeeded to the title; a younger son had died unmarried in 1670.

The new Earl buried his father with honours which would have befitted a Duke, a title which he felt had been unfairly withheld. This honour would yet come to the House of Cavendish, and sooner than anyone could have foreseen.

Revolution House at Whittington.

THE FOURTH EARL OF DEVONSHIRE
(PART I: 1640 - 1694)

By the time that the future Fourth Earl of Devonshire was born it had become a firm tradition to name the Cavendish heir William.

The fourth William Cavendish in line for the earldom was brought up against the background of the Civil War and completed his education with the Grand Tour of Europe. At the age of twenty-one he made his first move into political life upon his election as MP for Derby, in the same year that he acted as a train-bearer at the coronation of Charles II. A year later he was married, in Ireland, to Lady Mary Butler, the fifteen year-old daughter of the Duke of Ormonde. In 1665 Cavendish volunteered for service in the fleet and fought with credit alongside the Duke of York against the Dutch De Ruyter. The excitement of the encounter was very much to his liking, though the rest of his life was to be punctuated with more personal squabbles.

On the London scene William Cavendish was an extravagant philanderer, as handsome a rake as any man at Court. Such was his success with the ladies that the King forbade his mistress, Nell Gwynne, from keeping his company. On one occasion the roving courtier threw down the gauntlet in defence of the reputation of an actress. Both duellists emerged unscathed but the Cavendish second received an accidental blow from which he later died. In 1669 Cavendish managed to emerge with honour from a nasty incident in France when he was insulted by three Frenchmen at the opera. He returned the insult with a blow and immediately found himself at the sharp end of three swords. He had to be tugged away for his own safety but not before he had received a bad gash. His assailants were arrested but Cavendish, in an act of gentlemanly grace, gained their release.

Six years later he abandoned etiquette on greeting news of the death of a Colonel Howard with some satisfaction, on the grounds that the Colonel had once fought for France. The brother of the deceased published a broadsheet attacking Cavendish who, in defiance of a resolution passed in the House of Commons forbidding him to react, retaliated by posting a notice outside the Palace of Whitehall. It described Howard as a poltroon. Both men were committed to the Tower until they were calm enough to be reconciled.

EXECUTION AND MURDER

Behind these mild scandals, Cavendish had become increasingly active in parliament, a vigorous and fearless speaker in the House of Commons and a determined opponent of arbitrary government. He argued for strict adherence to annual parliaments and against the lax observance of anti-popery laws.

In 1677 he promoted a successful bill to recall English forces from service to the French crown and the following year served on the committee which drew up articles of impeachment against the Lord Treasurer Danby.

Whatever his views, Cavendish never agreed to any measure perceived as unbalanced in its fairness. Together with his old friend Lord Russell, he withdrew from the Privy Council in protest against the prevailing Roman Catholic interest. Cavendish went further, speaking out against King Charles' endeavours to preserve the right of succession for his Catholic brother, James, Duke of York. It is said that when Lord Russell was condemned to death for his part in a plot to assassinate James, Cavendish visited him in the condemned cell and suggested that they swop clothes to enable his friend to escape. Russell refused and was executed in 1683.

Around this time one of Cavendish's friends was murdered in Pall Mall and when it was discovered that the assailants were in the pay of the German Count Coningsmarck, Cavendish challenged him to a duel. He only withdrew the challenge on the direct insistence of the Secretary of State.

William Cavendish succeeded to the Devonshire title in 1684, two months before the death of Charles II. He took little trouble to hide his dislike and disapproval of the new King, James - a feeling that was mutual - but for a time national concerns had to be put aside as the result of another personal quarrel.

It came about when Colonel Thomas Culpepper, against a background of laying claims to lands in Derbyshire, questioned the Earl's allegiance to the Crown. Such a grave insult could have only one outcome, short of a duel, and Culpepper was felled to the ground. The Earl immediately made for Chatsworth to let the fuss die down but the Colonel went to gaol for eight months. The ill-feeling smouldered on until the two men came face-to-face again at Whitehall in the summer of 1687.

If it had not taken place outside the royal chambers, the caning of Colonel Culpepper would probably not have brought such wrath upon Devonshire. As it was the King was furious. Refusing a plea of parliamentary privilege he sent the Earl to prison until he could come up with the enormous fine of £30,000. James refused to accept bonds for twice that amount brought to him by the Dowager Countess of Devonshire - bonds signed by Charles I against money borrowed from the Cavendishes during the Civil War. Blaming the King for being blatantly difficult, the Earl discharged himself from gaol and fled to Chatsworth. He was careful to settle all debts for his prison 'lodgings' to avoid accusations of mere escape, and fled to Chatsworth.

Colourful stories have been told of how the Earl fled to Chatsworth ahead of a posse led by the Sheriff of Derby. Whether he was ever within reach or not, or whether he really did turn a key on the Sheriff, Devonshire remained above arrest and sent the King a promissory note for the £30,000.

BUILDER AND PLOTTER

The time proved to be opportune for attending to pressing matters at Chatsworth, nothing less than the rebuilding of the ill-proportioned, unstable house and the transformation of its gardens. The work was to continue almost up until the Earl's death.

Meanwhile, however, Devonshire grew increasingly concerned at the tyrannical behaviour of the King. He became involved in making secret and dangerous approaches to James's Protestant daughter, Mary, and her husband, Prince William of Orange, inviting them to de-throne the unpopular James. Hopes of achieving a Protestant succession were set back when in 1688 a son was born to James. William and Mary were pressed with a new urgency, the Earl of Devonshire adding his signature to a cipher letter sent to The Hague by a small group of eminent Englishmen. Devonshire, together with Lord Danby, the Earl of Delamere and Mr D'Arcy, met near Chesterfield to plot an uprising. Their meeting place was the parlour of the Cock and Pynot inn, today open to the public as the Revolution House.

The plan was for Prince William to land in the north, his route to London secured at York by Danby and at Nottingham by Devonshire. In the event William landed on the south coast. Devonshire, before marching to Nottingham to proclaim a well-received explanation of events, read his 'Declaration in Defence of the Protestant Religion' at Derby.

By the time William reached the capital, James had fled for France. Devonshire was kept in close attendance on William and Mary and remained prominent in securing their sovereignty. He stood firmly in their trust and at their coronation had the honour of bearing the crown when he acted as Lord High Steward of England.

Over the following years the Earl excelled as a skilled statesman. His patriotism and loyalty were accorded royal recognition when on 12 May 1694 he was created First Duke of Devonshire and Marquis of Hartington.

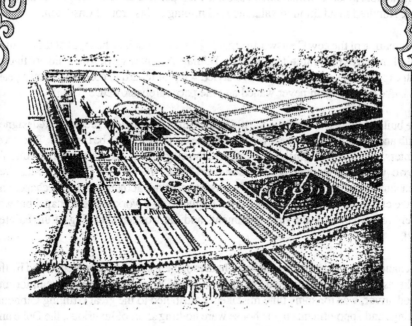

Chatsworth, showing the new South Front, Drawn 1699/70 by Kniff.

THE FIRST DUKE OF DEVONSHIRE
(Part II: 1694-1707)

When William Cavendish, Fourth Earl of Devonshire, was created First Duke of Devonshire, he was in his mid-fifties and could look back on his life with some satisfaction.

His relationship with William and Mary was, as might be expected, close. The matter of his unpaid debt to the exiled King James had been resolved; a committee of lords ruled that Devonshire's plea of peer's privilege had been wrongfully disallowed and, therefore, his committal had been illegal. The record of his conviction was deleted from the file of the exchequer and the promissory note was nullified - £30,000 was a huge sum, even to the house of Cavendish.

In fact the First Duke was spending on a vast scale, having embarked upon transforming Chatsworth House into the *'Palace of the Peak'*. The work needed all his considerable income, which since 1690 had incorporated the Crown rights of the High Peak Hundred in addition to valuable lead mining rights around Castleton.

The creation of the new Chatsworth arguably owed as much to the input of the cultured Duke himself as to his architect William Talman. Any new work which did not line up with expectations was undone and re-styled without regard to cost. For twenty years the Duke's enthusiasm never waned and the pace rarely slowed.

The building which arose from the old Elizabethan foundations presented redesigned south and east fronts and a new west front. The north was last to be finished. Two great painters were employed in the decoration of the magnificent rooms: the Italian Antonio Verrio who had worked at Windsor for Charles II, and the Versailles-inspired Frenchman, Louis Laguerre. Verrio's masterpieces are at their best in the chapel and on the ceiling of the State Dining Room. Laguerre also worked in the chapel but was solely responsible for the state apartments and the wonderful ceiling of the Painted Hall.

Outstanding English artists were brought in too, their workmanship recognized by the Duke as supreme in their field. Work by Samuel Watson, the Heanor sculptor and woodcarver, was for some time mistakenly attributed to the great Grinling Gibbons. Fittings and appointments in the house were nothing short of luxurious; the Duke and Duchess had a marble bath with hot and cold running water, as well as flushing water closets with marble bowls.

In the parkland, ambitious landscaping involved the removal of a hill to open up the southerly aspect, then a canal was constructed across the site. A stately formality was imposed on wild nature when it came to the gardens, laid out with avenues, parterres, a bowling green, fountains and the splendid cascade. The end result, as described by the present Duchess of Devonshire in her book *The House, A Portrait of Chatsworth* reflects 'all that was best in the golden age of architecture'.

EXTRAVAGANT AND INDEPENDENT

Throughout the years of his rebuilding of Chatsworth, the Duke continued to enjoy the London lifestyle, with an extravagance which for a time almost got out of hand. On one occasion £1,000 was spent on a masked ball and concert at Kensington. The Duke also gambled huge sums at the races and cock fights, yet he spared £500 to give to Greenwich Hospital.

Politically he held on to his independent views, prepared to stand apart whenever he disagreed with official Whig policy. At least the pride which formerly led him into duels and arguments was now satisfied with redress at law. A number of lawsuits went his way in the 1690s, at least two arising from horse racing disputes and one concerning

20

hunting rights in the Needwood Forest, of which he was Ranger.

After the death of Queen Mary, the King spent very little time in England and the Duke of Devonshire was one of three lords Justices who stood in to administer the Kingdom. In 1702 on the accession of Queen Anne, to whom as a princess Devonshire had offered safety and hospitality at the height of the Glorious Revolution, he was confirmed in all his offices. He served as lord High Steward at the coronation. Although for a time unfounded rumours of treasonable inclinations put a strain on the royal trust, the Duchess of Devonshire remained in the Queen's close circle of friends.

BIRTH AND DEATH

The Duchess was a woman of tact and patience, qualities never attributed to her husband. She was also as virtuous as he was not, though well aware of his infidelities throughout their married life. The Duke had fathered a number of illegitimate children, the last at the age of sixty-five on a teenaged actress whom he had established in a property near his London home, Devonshire House in Piccadilly.

Four months after the birth, his paramour died. The Duke paid for her funeral and had his infant daughter brought to be cared for at Devonshire House. A codicil to his will left £10,000 to the child on her majority or marriage. The death of his young mistress greatly distressed the ageing Duke, already suffering painful and worsening bouts of illness. At Devonshire House on 18 August of the following year, 1707, he died of 'the stone and strangury'.

The body of the First Duke of Devonshire was conveyed in great state to the City and thence to Derby for burial at All Saints Church, now the Cathedral. Of his surviving legitimate children his namesake, William, succeeded to the title.

Chatsworth and village of Edensor.

THE SECOND DUKE OF DEVONSHIRE
(1673-1729)

Whether Earl or Duke, each successor to the Devonshire title seemed to inherit the personality traits not of his father but of his paternal grandfather. It was as though the title and wealth was destined to fall, alternately, between extravagant extrovert and staid caretaker.

The pattern continued with William Cavendish, Second Duke of Devonshire, cautious and responsible and perfectly suited to guard his valuable inheritance. Though unlike his father in manner, he nevertheless shared both his political astuteness and a deep commitment to the upkeep of Chatsworth. Both men recognised that the two interests were inextricably linked, in that without political influence families such as theirs would be weakened by the advancing changes in England's social structure. Some degree of political power was already filtering 'down' to the middle classes.

As Lord Hartington, the future Second Duke had married Rachel Russell, the fourteen year-old daughter of William, Lord Russell. Of staunch Whig stock, Hartington became MP for Derbyshire during his father's lifetime; his younger brother, Lord James, went on to represent Derby for over forty years. At the end of the 17th century the Tories held a considerable degree of power, with the security of great Whig families like the Devonshires resting largely on events at Westminster. Hartington was well aware of his responsibilities in this respect and thus was an experienced politician by the time he inherited his title in 1707.

SOCIAL PATRONAGE

Queen Anne had already appointed him Captain of the Yeomen of the Guard and now gave him his father's old post as Steward of the Household, proof enough that his loyalty to the monarchy outweighed her own Tory affiliations.

By this time the Duke had become a firm friend of Robert Walpole, with whom he had jointly been returned to the safe Whig seat of Castle Rising, Devonshire having lost his Derbyshire seat. The ideals of the two men were matched exactly and although Devonshire was himself an accomplished orator, he was outshone by Walpole. Yet Devonshire possessed what that outstanding and ambitious parliamentarian lacked - noble breeding.

Without the friendship and social patronage of the Duke, Robert Walpole would not have been accepted by the close-knit, aristocratic and very wealthy young Whigs. Yet his welcome into their London clubs, such as the Kit-Cat Club, was vital to his political career and thus to the eventual rise to power of Walpole and the whole Whig party. First, however, difficult times lay ahead. Towards the end of her reign, intrigues at Court led to Queen Anne's deep antagonism towards the Whig administration. She dismissed their ministry in 1710 and the new parliament was returned with a Tory majority. Devonshire was removed from his Stewardship and ordered to return his staff of office which, deeply affronted, he did with obvious ill grace. Anne had aimed to end the domination of the Whigs, yet when the Tories came to power she left a number of Whigs in their posts in an endeavour to break up the party system. The Duke of Devonshire, though, was unable to obtain even an audience with her.

Unlike the ailing Queen, however, the Whigs had time on their side. They were also certain of a complete reversal of fortunes under the Hanoverian succession which lay ahead; from fifteen pregnancies the Queen had no surviving children and it had been Devonshire who had introduced a bill to settle precedence on the son of the Elector of Hanover. Thus the Protestant succession - which the First Duke of Devonshire had helped to secure through the Glorious Revolution - would be assured.

Queen Anne, meanwhile, was approaching the end of her reign. The Duke of Devonshire removed himself to Chatsworth and awaited her death, which came in 1714. The new King, George I, Elector of Hanover, inevitably attached himself to the Whigs, appointing Devonshire as one of the Lords Justice to act in his name until he arrived in England. Whig dominance was regained and in particular the aristocracy could be sure that their property and wealth was protected for the foreseeable future.

TREASURES FOR CHATSWORTH

Robert Walpole was now on course for political greatness. As First Lord of the Treasury and Chancellor of the Exchequer he became, in effect, the first 'prime minister' of Britain. He and Devonshire continued to share the same loyal friendship

23

and political causes of old.

It was, of course, largely with Chatsworth in mind that Devonshire was so committed to Whig ideals. His palatial family seat had been only recently - and expensively - rebuilt when it passed to him, but the Second Duke was to enrich the great house in befitting style. He had been a steady and serious collector of European works of art all his adult life, demonstrating an unerring eye for outstanding drawings and paintings which became, almost incidentally, excellent long-term investments. Fashion never dictated his personal choice, for instance his interest in Old Master drawings was shared by only a few other collectors at that time. In fact his major contribution to the treasures of Chatsworth proved to be the great collection of Old Master drawings assembled by Finck, son of a former pupil of Rembrandt. The addition of various prints and engravings, as well as a number of Old Masters, may also be attributed to the Second Duke. He is known too to have purchased Greek and Roman carved gems and was a keen collector of coins.

Devonshire continued in favour at Court until the end of his life, having earned the close trust of George, Prince of Wales, who came to the throne in 1727. The Second Duke died two years later and the title passed to his elder son, William Cavendish. Lord Charles, the younger son, was the future father of Henry Cavendish, the famous scientist.

Eyam Rectory. Drawing by Kenneth Steele, reproduced by courtesy of Davy-Ashmore Ltd., Sheffield.

THE THIRD DUKE OF DEVONSHIRE
(1698-1755)

Like his predecessors, this William Cavendish was brought up to be aware of how his class depended on social and political stability. But because he lived in times that favoured aristocratic Whig families - due in great measure to the political activities of his own father and grandfather, the First and Second Dukes of Devonshire - this Cavendish heir had no real inclination towards politics. As Lord Hartington he did serve as MP for Lostwithiel and when he inherited his title, in 1729, was rather taken under the wing of his late father's old friend, Sir Robert Walpole.

As Third Duke of Devonshire he was appointed Lord Steward of the Royal Household. Then Walpole set him up as Lord Privy Seal and, in 1737, as Viceroy of Ireland. The Duke kept this lucrative position for three years, well suited to the role and popular with the Irish people.

Variously described as 'plain in his manners, negligent in his dress.. lazy .. homespun .. bluff', Devonshire possessed a steady reliability which was praised by Dr Johnson: 'He was not a man of superior abilities, but he was a man strictly faithful to his word. If, for instance, he had promised you an acorn, and none had grown that year in his woods, he would not have contented himself with that excuse; he would have sent to Denmark for it. So unconditional was he in keeping his word...'

A less generous critic was the gossipy Horace Walpole, son of Robert, who sniped that 'The Duke's outside was unpolished, his inside unpolishable'. True the Duke was a heavy drinker and an avid gambler but it was his Duchess who really came in for some snobbish criticism.

FAMILY LIFE

She had been born Katherine Hoskyns, daughter of a wealthy businessman with no claim to noble breeding. It so happened that when the future Duke, as Lord Hartington, took her for his wife, he was plagued by large gambling debts which had escalated since he left Oxford. For the down-to-earth heiress and her father, 'Miser' Hoskyns, there were no qualms about merging her fortune with a title.

By 1720 the Hartingtons had an heir, William, to be followed by three brothers and three sisters. Family life was close-knit and homely with the children given 'pet' names: Guts, Gundy, Mrs Hopeful, Mrs Tiddle, Puss, Cat and Toe. Even after Katherine became Duchess of Devonshire, she presided over an easy-going household. Horace Walpole may have described her as 'delightfully vulgar' but when the Devonshires did entertain, guests were relaxed and their conversation informal.

The Third Duke undertook few changes at Chatsworth but in 1733 he had to commission William Kent to rebuild Devonshire House in Piccadilly after it burned down. Kent also designed new furniture, most of which is now at Chatsworth, as are two portraits by Van Dyck presented to the Duke by Horace Walpole.

Little occurred to disturb the Devonshires until their peace was suddenly shattered early in 1748, when 'Guts' Hartington set his heart on marriage to sixteen-year-old Charlotte Boyle, sole heiress to the very rich Third Earl of Burlington. She was in line to inherit two mansions in London, Bolton Abbey in Yorkshire and estates in Londesborough and Ireland.

To some, though, the Burlington ancestry was flawed by its descent from Richard Boyle. In the reign of Elizabeth I, Boyle had taken advantage of the stricken Sir Walter Raleigh - soon to be executed - by purchasing estates from him at bargain prices.

It was also widely known that the Third Earl of Burlington maintained an enduring and intimate relationship with architect William Kent, whilst Lady Burlington was the long-standing mistress of the Duke of Grafton. Worse still, Charlotte's elder sister,

Dorothy, had died at the age of seventeen after rumoured ill-treatment from her husband. He was Lord Euston, who happened to be the son of the Duke of Grafton. This account of the scandal was published eighty years later amongst the recollections of Elizabeth, second wife of the Fifth Duke of Devonshire.

'Lady Dorothy ... married a man she adored and of the first rank, but he was a man of vicious principles and in love with his brother's wife. He promised her, so it is said, that no son of his would inherit his father's fortune and when Lady Euston was with child, he drove her through the worst paved streets of London. He made her walk till exhausted. She had been seen to sit fainting on the steps before peoples' houses... When Lady Euston was in labour he suffered none but the midwife to come and after her death - she died in labour the same thing. The birth was premature and the child died.'

UNHAPPY DIFFERENCES

Whatever the reason for her disapproval of Charlotte Boyle, the Duchess of Devonshire would insist only that the girl was too young to marry her very eligible son. Although the Duke probably favoured the match, above all he wanted peace and quiet. For once, however, he could not retire into his complacent shell and, against his nature, was drawn into a bitter family feud. He would have been happy for either his wife or their son to concede defeat but there was to be no compromise.

Finally a private wedding was held on 28 March 1748 in London, hosted by the Burlingtons. The Duke of Devonshire attended but the Duchess stayed away; by the time her husband returned to Chatsworth she had moved out and into the rectory at Eyam. The new groom and his father made constant efforts to restore good relations but were rebuffed. By this time the Duchess was directing her distress at the Duke, writing to him: 'my abhorrence to this most Cursed Match increases more and more every day I live and has made such unhappy differences amongst us.'

It took over a year of persuasion to bring the Duchess back to Chatsworth. Horace Walpole wrote to tell a friend in June 1749 how the Duke had resigned from his position as Lord Steward of the Royal Household 'for the unaccountable and unenvied pleasure of shutting himself up at Chatsworth with his ugly mad Duchess; the more extraordinary sacrifice, as he turned her head, rather than give up a favourite match for his son.' From this time the Devonshires distanced themselves from Court life. As Walpole had inferred, there were whispers that the Duchess had lost her reason. For the Duke, whose great passions were still gambling and drinking, being cut off at Chatsworth left him with little to live for and he died in 1755.

Yet he had lived long enough to see the untimely death of Charlotte and the attendant vast increase in Cavendish wealth. As for his Duchess, she not only outlived her husband and her unacceptable daughter-in-law but also her own son, William, the Fourth Duke of Devonshire.

Paine's Bridge. From "Chatsworth" by Llewellyn Jewitt.

THE FOURTH DUKE OF DEVONSHIRE
(1720-1764)

By the time that William Cavendish succeeded to the title of Fourth Duke of Devonshire in 1755, he had been widowed and left with four young children. Aloof and polite where his father had been cordial and easy-going, he was never to remarry. It was only in his later years that he became reconciled with his mother, who had been so opposed to his marriage - which against her predictions had turned out to be a very happy match.

The untimely death of the young Lady Hartington had brought the Burlington inheritance to the House of Cavendish, making the Fourth Duke one of the wealthiest men in England. Lord Burlington's exceptional library of architectural books and drawings came to Chatsworth although the new Duke took no interest in adding to the Devonshire collections or works of art.

Yet he did bring sweeping changes to the appearance of his Derbyshire seat. By pulling down stables and offices at the original, west entrance to Chatsworth House and making that front the new facade, he 'reversed' the direction in which the house faced. The architect James Paine was engaged to design both new stables and the graceful bridge over the Derwent, the course of the river having just been altered.

Much of the village of Edensor was demolished and rebuilt out of sight of the House. Lancelot 'Capability' Brown was employed to replace the First Duke's formal gardens with a more fashionable natural garden, as well as laying out the magnificent enclosed park as far as the ducal eye could see. In the middle of the 18th century, Chatsworth was already a tourist attraction. Monday was 'public day' when visitors could tour the State Apartments and gardens.

'CROWN PRINCE OF THE WHIGS'

The Fourth Duke also had political business to attend to. Shortly after succeeding to his title he was given the Governorship of Ireland. The post brought a very favourable remuneration for the effort involved and his title as Lord of the Boyle estates and Governor of Cork helped to assure his acceptance by the Irish people.

The Cavendish family was described by Horace Walpole as 'almost a political party of their own' and had four seats in parliament. Devonshire had cut his political teeth as soon as he came of age, being first returned as MP for Derbyshire in 1741. He was respected as an intelligent and honourable politician, though actually referred to in royal circles as 'Crown Prince of the Whigs' for his regal manner. Yet his political endeavours were self-interested only in so far as he could work to preserve the status quo of the whole Whig aristocracy.

National events were to take him to higher office than he had ambition towards. Following the outbreak of the Seven Years' War with France in 1756 the country suffered heavy losses and the policies of the Whig government took the blame. The party's parliamentary power was under serious threat and the great Whig families were deeply alarmed.

Their champion and a long-term holder of ministerial office was the Duke of Newcastle but even Whigs could see that he was not the man to save the country. By popular demand that role was handed to William Pitt. Newcastle resigned as Secretary of State and was excluded from Pitt's new ministry, the two men then being on bad terms. Pitt turned instead to the only prominent Whig whom nobody could fault - the Duke of Devonshire.

AS PRIME MINISTER

On 16 November 1756, Devonshire was appointed Prime Minister with Pitt as his Secretary of State. Accepting that his role was nominal, the Duke was happy to leave

Pitt free to conduct war policy and remained in office for only six months. In May 1757 Pitt took up the premiership himself and the Duke of Devonshire became Lord Chamberlain, a post which suited him well.

Pitt's leadership brought British victories in the Seven Years' War but George III, who had come to the throne in 1760, was resolved on seeing the country at peace and refused to back his strategies. Pitt resigned in October 1761 and Newcastle took his place. The young King did not intend this to last. Backed by his chief adviser, Lord Bute, George III had a deep dislike of Whigs and was determined to end the power of the old Whig families. The Dukes of Newcastle and Devonshire were high on his list.

After seven months Newcastle was removed from office to make way for Bute. The Duke of Devonshire found himself in an intolerable position; his integrity made it impossible to remain as Lord Chamberlain under a committed anti-Whig Prime Minister.

Yet Devonshire felt that the historical links between his family and the throne entitled him to every respect and he would not be humiliated into giving up his office. Coolly indignant, he left for Chatsworth and did not return to London to take part in any councils throughout the summer of 1762.

THE GOLDEN KEY

In the month of October he received a message from the King, summoning him to attend a Council convened to discuss peace negotiations with France. But Devonshire, whose health had not been good for some time, took a long diversion to take the waters at Bath before proceeding to London. In a pique the King rudely refused to see him, whereupon Devonshire found a way both to teach him good manners and to keep his own self respect. Before he could be commanded to do so, the Duke voluntarily gave up his golden key - his symbol of office, together with his staff. He returned immediately to Chatsworth.

King George had been cheated of a petty victory but the Devonshires had lost what almost amounted to a birthright - the assurance of a prestigious role in parliament. Yet they had been firm monarchists and the actions of the King were seen as ill-advised. Commiserations sent to Devonshire by the Duke of Cumberland, actually a member of the royal family, were typical of the many messages he received: 'Our family must not be left long without a Duke of Devonshire in the Administration.'

In spite of such support, the Fourth Duke felt that he had failed to consolidate the political achievements of his ancestors. His state of health grew steadily worse and in the autumn of 1764 he went to Spa, in Belgium, for the curative waters. It was there in October that he died after suffering two strokes. His son and heir was another William, only 15 years old.

The Crescent at Buxton, from "The Gem of the Peak" by Adam, 1843.

THE FIFTH DUKE OF DEVONSHIRE
(1748-1811)

Bereaved of his mother at the age of six and left to inherit the Dukedom nine years later on the death of his father, William Cavendish was a joyless and uncommunicative young man.

Disinterested in political life, which after all had taken its toll on the health of his father, the Fifth Duke found everything else dull too. All his life he was weighed down by what has been described as constitutional apathy'. Even in his youth he put no effort into socialising other than heavy drinking and gambling, rarely having to rouse himself far from his London home, Devonshire House in Piccadilly.

Wealthier than any man needed to be, Devonshire had no need of good looks. Indolence kept him plump in the face and corpulent in body. Yet if the man of his portrait looks as much boring as bored, at least his expression might as easily reflect his gentle and long-suffering character.

In his mid-twenties, an undemanding affair with 'a tarnished Mayfair milliner called Charlotte Spencer' (*Stags and Serpents*: John Pearson) gave the Duke his first child, a daughter. Born in 1774 and named Charlotte, she was given the surname Williams as a discreet acknowledgement to her paternity.

It was far more important for the Duke to father a legitimate heir and to this end he selected a very acceptable bride. Over many years the Cavendishes had maintained a friendship with the Spencers of Althorp and, as more recent history has confirmed, the Spencers have produced very eligible offspring.

Earl Spencer's oldest daughter was Georgiana, full of life, warm and impulsive. When she learned that the undemonstrative Devonshire had put himself forward as her suitor she fell in love with an exuberance and emotion that was quite one-sided. No matter; on 5 June 1774, within days of her 17th birthday, Georgiana and the Duke were married.

CANIS, MRS. RAT & RACKY

The sparkling young Duchess enchanted everyone she met, even the grumpy George III. She took society by storm and set up court at Devonshire House, at the core of the fashionable 'New Whigs' set. Only her own husband was impassive to her spontaneous affection, which somehow endured an early miscarriage and eight years of childlessness. Georgiana apparently tried to counter her unhappiness by gambling. This was to become a lifelong addiction and her losses were phenomenal.

Then in the spring of 1782 an inexplicable element animated the Devonshire marriage in the feline form of Lady Elizabeth Foster, known as Bess. She was the same age as Georgiana and from the moment she entered their lives the three of them became devoted to one another. Soon Bess was addressing the couple by the pet names Canis and Mrs Rat. She herself was Racky.

Relaxed in the new, warmer atmosphere around her, Georgiana finally completed a successful pregnancy and in July 1783 gave birth to a daughter, Georgiana Dorothy. The following year she caused a lively scandal when she and her friends took to the poorer streets of London in active support of Charles James Fox in the general election. The ladies dazzled the people with their extravagant finery, carried voters to the hustings in their grand carriages and even bought stubborn votes with kisses. Fox's victory was assured.

Nothing indicates that the Duke ever resented living in his wife's shadow, he was too lethargic to spare the effort for either debate or action himself. Yet he finally proved that he had a heart; by this time, and apparently without acrimony from Georgiana, Bess was sharing both the family home and the loving embraces of 'Canis'.

The me´nage a` trois was soon extended. In the summer of 1785, only two weeks apart,

Georgiana gave birth to Harriet and Bess to Caroline, given the surname St Jules.

The Devonshires still had no legitimate heir but neither was in glowing health. As well as chronic headaches, made worse by worry over her ever-escalating debts, Georgiana suffered from a liver complaint. As for the Duke, he was advised by his doctor, Erasmus Darwin, to cut his alcohol intake by half. Darwin explained: 'this inflammation of the liver, occasion'd originally by drinking much spiritous or fermented liquor .. causes the gout.'

Bess, meanwhile, was alluring, cheerful - and soon pregnant again. In May 1787 she presented the Duke with his first son, Augustus William Clifford.

AN HEIR

For the Duchess to be well enough to produce an heir, Bess suggested she forsake the gambling tables and distance herself from her debtors. So it was that in June 1789 the trio left for Europe. On a visit to Marie Antoinette at Versailles they witnessed the first alarming stirrings of the French Revolution. The party moved on to Spa and here Georgiana finally conceived the healthy, precious son who was born on 21 May 1790, William Spencer Cavendish.

The household settled down again in London and there, for the first time in her life, Georgiana was unfaithful, besotted by the handsome Charles Grey, future Prime Minister. Georgiana became pregnant, Grey made himself scarce and the normally unemotional Duke banished his wife to France, where in February 1792 she handed over her newborn daughter to be brought up by Grey's family.

Not until September 1793 was Georgiana allowed back to her husband and children. He showed rare pleasure in the reunion, of which Georgiana wrote to her mother: 'The Duke has the gout, but looks pretty well. There was never anything equal to the attention I have met from him - to the generosity and kindness.'

The me´nage a` trois was resumed, their life of happy domesticity increasingly spent at Chatsworth. The Devonshires had spent many summers there since the early years of their marriage, occasionally holding open days at the great house, when any visitors would be invited to dinner.

It was from Derbyshire in 1778 that the Duke, as Lord Lieutenant of the county, had led the Derbyshire militia to Kent en route to face the French.

COUNTRY HOME

Now in his forties, the Duke was content to let Georgiana and Bess run Chatsworth as a country home for their children: the five they had borne him, as well as Charlotte Williams and Bess's two teenaged sons of her own failed marriage. These two boys

33

were educated at Oxford at the Duke's expense.

The private apartments of Chatsworth had been decorated in the latest French fashion. French craftsmen were commissioned to make some of the pieces which still furnish the Yellow Drawing Room. The architect John Carr was brought in to design furniture for the Blue Drawing Room but he is better known in the Peak for his elegant Crescent at Buxton. It is said that it was built from the profits of the Duke's copper mines at Ecton.

Before long there were deep concerns about Georgiana's health. Her agonising headaches worsened and she was left blind in one eye from a disfiguring eye infection, at the same time suffering a great deal of pain from gallstones. She still had some £40,000 of debts kept secret from her husband.

She played one last role as Queen of the Foxite Whigs when, upon the death of Pitt early in 1806, many of her old circle were appointed to Fox's new ministry. Georgiana gave them a large supper party at Devonshire House; the Duke had been offered his choice of post but was not interested.

Within weeks Georgiana fell into her final illness and on 30 March died of 'an abcess on the liver'. On the day that her coffin left for Derbyshire to be buried in the family vault, the Duke took to his room and spoke to no-one.

Bess continued to live with him although she had never been liked by Georgiana's children - young Lord Hartington referred to her as 'a crocodile'. Nevertheless, in October 1809 the Duke made her his second wife. He had only another two years to live, dying without fuss or drama of dropsy in August 1811.

Edensor in the early days of the 6th. Duke.

THE SIXTH DUKE OF DEVONSHIRE
(1790-1858)

In contrast to his father who married twice, William Spencer Compton Cavendish would always be known as the Bachelor Duke.

As Lord Hartington he completed his education at Trinity College, Cambridge and by the age of sixteen was already receiving friends and holding dinner parties at Chatsworth for budding society beauties and college friends. He later referred to these years as 'my life's golden time' and recalled with fond humour his father's response when his agent complained that young Hartington was spending large sums of money: 'So much the better, Mr. Heaton; he will have a great deal to spend'.

His father's lax attitude towards finances and the gross extravagance of Duchess Georgiana were, unfortunately, combined in their son, who completely disregarded the debts inherited along with his titles in 1811.

An insight into his personality comes from *The House, A Portrait of Chatsworth*, by the present Duchess of Devonshire: 'It is his sense of humour which makes one love him more than all the rest put together. He was funny and sad, the irresistible combination which is one of the secrets of charm.' He was fondly known as 'Hart' to those who knew him, including King George IV, who coined the word 'undevonshirelike' as a mild reproval to others.

In 1825 the Sixth Duke represented his King and country on an embassy to Russia for the coronation of Tsar Nicholas, with such grandeur that he had to top up the government allowance with £50,000 out of his own pocket. This tribute did not go unnoticed by the Tsar; even before he conferred honours on Devonshire, Britain and Russia had signed a formal treaty of alliance.

In London, Devonshire House had come back to life under the hospitable and free-spending Duke, who hosted concerts and splendid receptions unmatched in the capital. Yet despite all his society connections he never fell in love. For about ten years from 1828, however, he discreetly kept a mistress named Elizabeth Warwick, first in London and later at The Rookery at Ashford-in-the-Water.

As regards an heir, Devonshire was more than happy to leave his estates to his beloved niece, Blanche, and her husband William Cavendish, Lord Burlington - a great-grandson of the Third Duke. In 1833 the couple produced a healthy son so the succession looked safe for a further generation.

To her uncle's great grief, Blanche died before the age of thirty. He wrote to her widower in desolation: 'You are my heir. Be as if my son... Let my houses be your home and the home of your children'. But Burlington felt it better not to accept.

ROYAL CONNECTIONS

During the preceding years Devonshire had taken an untypical interest in politics, supporting the Reform proposals of Prime Minister Lord Grey. The majority of the aristocracy saw Reform as a threat to their interests and ignored the increasingly insistent voice - and rioting - of the people. Finally the King, who liked Devonshire and trusted his advice, made it clear to the House of Lords that he would countenance their opposition no longer.

Peaceful political change was assured and with this, Devonshire retired from political life.

He was not an enthusiastic courtier either, though had served as Lord Chamberlain to George IV and William IV. A portrait of George IV by Lawrence and the coronation chairs of William IV and Queen Adelaide were gifts which he brought back to Chatsworth House.

Princess Victoria stayed at Chatsworth in 1832, attending her first 'grown up' dinner there. She returned eleven years later as Queen. The Duke, of course, gave her a magnificent welcome on both occasions.

In 1844 he made lavish preparations for a visit from Tsar Nicholas, in whose honour the Emperor Fountain - the tallest in the world - was built. In the event the Tsar never came to Chatsworth but visited his old friend at his Chiswick villa instead.

'THIS MOST BEAUTIFUL HOUSE'

The Sixth Duke had never ceased to delight in what he called 'this most beautiful house' and added extensively to the collections, his great passions being sculptures and books. He was well versed in English literature and in 1812 bought the library of the Bishop of Ely for £10,000. Another major purchase was the collection of 1,347 volumes of plays assembled by John Kemble. The largely scientific library of Henry Cavendish, the 'genius of Clapham', also came to Chatsworth.

In 1819 Devonshire made his first journey to Italy, accompanied by the architect Jeffry Wyatt - later Sir Jeffry Wyatville. Numerous works of art were brought back from this and other travels overseas: furniture, rare Italian marbles, Roman antiquities, busts and sculptures - including Canova's masterpiece Endymion. From Moscow came draperies of Chinese silk and from Messina a pair of horns charmed from an innkeeper.

The trip to Italy and the Vatican inspired the Duke to employ Wyatt to greatly extend the frontage of Chatsworth House with a new wing surmounted by a tower and belvedere.

Devonshire often purchased pieces on impulse. On one such occasion he was passing a London saleroom while an auction was in progress. He went inside and immediately set about bidding for piece after piece of unique old oak carvings, on view to the public in the Oak Room still, just as he would have wished.

For the Sixth Duke was just as happy to show his treasures to passers-by as to royalty and acquaintances like the Duke of Wellington and Charles Dickens. In his day a notice of 1841 hung in the Tapestry Gallery regretting that 'In wet and dirty weather parties of no more than 8 persons may see the principal apartments'.

In 1844 Devonshire penned his Handbook to Chatsworth and Hardwick in which he described the extensive changes he had made at Chatsworth. Quite clearly he was very proud of his properties and had put careful thought into all the alterations.

The marble flooring of the Painted Hall had been relaid whilst elsewhere a new pavement of ancient marbles was laid by a workman sent from Rome. Tiling of another was copied from mosaic floors excavated at Pompeii. The Duke also brought in '2 or 3 bearded artists in blouses' from Paris to update the decoration of his lower Library, home to almost 6,000 volumes.

Devonshire was also an avid collector of minerals. As a boy he had learned about mineralogy from the famous White Watson of Bakewell, who had helped the Duchess Georgiana to keep her collection in order. Her son made further additions, on one occasion taking Derbyshire and Cornish ores to St. Petersburg to exchange for foreign ones.

Like his ancestor Bess of Hardwick, the Sixth Duke held local workmanship and materials in high regard too. Specimens of Blue John were made up into a window and he employed Ashford marble and the rare 'Duke's red' for decorative work. He had oriental porphyry repolished at Ashford marble mills for his sculpture gallery, where Derbyshire marble was used for pedestals and doorcases and Chatsworth.stone for the walls.

PAXTON'S FLAIR

From 1826 Devonshire had been helped with the transformation of his gardens by Joseph Paxton. He was responsible in great measure for the present appearance of Chatsworth including the great Emperor Fountain. As usual costs were no object and Paxton's gardens became a magnificent complement to the House. Ten years after his arrival he started work on his colossal conservatory and the Duke began to finance botanical expeditions to fill it with exotic plants. The two men had become close friends and in 1838 spent a year travelling abroad in search of species to bring home. On their return their next venture was the remodelling of Edensor. Each house was provided with running water and the villagers had a school, playground, a drying ground and fields to graze their own cows. The delighted inhabitants duly named their landlord the 'Good Duke'.

Yet his endless expenditure, coupled with the repayment of old debts, was in fact out of all proportion to his income. The day of reckoning came in 1844 when he was forced into facing the disastrous state of his accounts; there was no choice but to sell off large parts of the estates.

His two beloved homes, Chatsworth and Hardwick, remained untouched and there was no need either to make further savings. Devonshire could continue to enjoy life in style, whether in Derbyshire or London.

His health remained good until he suffered a stroke in his early sixties from which he recovered quite well. It was during a stay at Hardwick in the New Year of 1858 that he was taken ill again and died peacefully in his bed in the early hours of January 18th.

The Great Conservatory, taken from "Chatsworth" by Llewellyn Jewitt

THE SEVENTH DUKE OF DEVONSHIRE (1808-1891)

As a grandson of Lord George Cavendish, brother of the Fifth Duke Of Devonshire, William Cavendish - and Earl of Burlington of the second creation - came in line for the Devonshire title after the death of the Bachelor Duke.

Cavendish was scholarly and intelligent. At the age of twenty-eight he had become Chancellor of London University and subsequently Chancellor of Cambridge, where as a student he had excelled at mathematics. In the early 1830s he also represented Cambridge University as a Reformist Whig MP and in later life donated £6,300 to the University to build and equip a laboratory of experimental physics in honour of the scientist Henry Cavendish. The Cavendish Laboratory is noted for its prestigious work to this day.

William Cavendish married Lady Blanche Howard, herself a granddaughter of the Fifth Duke of Devonshire and Duchess Georgiana. Blanche's first son died in infancy but she bore three healthy sons and a daughter before her own sudden and early death. Her husband mourned her deeply for the rest of his life and never remarried. He tutored their children personally to give them a close family life, his own father having been killed in a carriage accident in 1812.

At the age of fifty Cavendish took up his ducal inheritance but without Blanche to share it he felt himself to be little more than its financial guardian. To his dismay portents of disaster were evident from his first glance at the accounts. His Burlington holdings, which included Eastbourne and land around the Lancashire coastline, were not entirely free of debt either and he had already moved into the world of investment and commerce.

It was fortuitous, therefore, that the Seventh Duke of Devonshire actually preferred the sober world of business to the extravagant socialising of his predecessors. Acting as his own accountant, arguably the best in his line since Bess of Hardwick, Devonshire took immediate steps to reduce the massive expenses and outgoings which had so reduced the vast income.

All rents were reviewed and updated and the large payroll was pruned, which at Chatsworth meant farewell to Sir Joseph Paxton, no longer the unknown gardener who had come to work for the Sixth Duke but the world famous architect of the Crystal Palace at the heart of the British Empire.

Meanwhile Devonshire turned his thoughts to securing and even enhancing his inheritance through long term investment in industry. He put money into the expansion of the Lancashire docklands and harbours and, following the discovery of iron-ore near his small village of Barrow, supervised its transformation into an industrial giant. The small fishing community of Eastbourne grew into a select seaside resort after Devonshire built modern roads, hotels, shops and houses.

In a different vein, the Seventh Duke founded the Royal Agricultural Society and achieved personal success with his prize-winning herd of Holker Shorthorns. Holker Hall in Lancashire was his favourite home, though at Chatsworth he had the great library catalogued and also appointed Sir Gilbert Scott to rebuild Edensor church. Chatsworth House had become a mecca for day trippers as soon as the railway had reached Rowsley; 11,000 visitors came in Whit Week 1884.

By this time Devonshire had suffered another grievous loss. At the beginning of 1882 his heir, Lord Hartington, was Secretary of State for India and his second son, Lord Frederick, was financial secretary to the Treasury. In the early part of that year Prime Minister Gladstone, seeking to deal with violence in Ireland through conciliation, offered the post of Chief Secretary for Ireland to Hartington - the Devonshire estates in Lismore gave the family a close interest in events in Ireland. Hartington turned down the post but to the deep concern of their father, it was taken up by his 'beloved Freddie'.

When Lord Frederick left for Dublin in the first week of May 1882 he carried a message of peace from Gladstone, yet within hours of its delivery the bearer was dead. This report appeared in an English newspaper:

The murder of Lord Frederick Cavendish and Mr. Burke.

'All England thrilled with horror when the news arrived that the Chief Secretary, Lord F. Cavendish, and Under Secretary, Mr. Burke, for Ireland, had been foully murdered in Phoenix Park, Dublin. On May 6th Lord Cavendish - who had only been eight hours in Dublin - was walking through the park to the Secretary's Lodge accompanied by Mr. Burke. When within sight of the vice-regal grounds, a car drove rapidly up on which four men and the driver were seated. When the secretaries were reached, the car stopped, and the four men immediately descended, and attacked the unfortunate gentlemen with long knives or daggers. A terrible struggle ensued but, unarmed and assailed by four, the officials were stabbed to death. Their fiendish deed accomplished, the four murderers returned to their car and rapidly drove away. The victims were conveyed to the hospital but life was extinct in each.'

Cavendish's body was brought back for burial at Edensor. The Prime Minister and many MPs travelled from London for the funeral and Queen Victoria sent a wreath of everlasting flowers. It was said that over a quarter of a million mourners lined the route taken by the cortege through Chatsworth Park.

The Duke of Devonshire was devastated and his melancholy worsened with the inexorable failure of his industrial ventures. In spite of all his earnest efforts few had brought lasting success, even Barrow had been hit by a continuing drop in demand for steel. Matters reached the point where Devonshire estates in Ireland had to be used as security for a debt of £80,000 to the Scottish Widows Insurance Company.

In 1891 Devonshire was bereaved yet again upon the death of his youngest son, Lord Edward Cavendish, father of three boys. This was the final blow for the sad old Duke and in the last month of the year he too passed away whilst in residence at Holker Hall.

The 8th. Duke in 1877.

THE EIGHTH DUKE OF DEVONSHIRE
(1833-1908)

Spencer Compton Cavendish was born at Holker Hall in Lancashire, the oldest of four children who were left motherless in 1840. Their widowed father, remembering his miserable schooldays at Eton, kept the children at home and taught them himself.

At the age of eighteen, Spencer Compton - known as 'Cav' - went on to Trinity College, Cambridge, where to the concern of his deeply religious father he enjoyed an understated 'little wildness'. He became a familiar figure at Newmarket where he developed a lifelong love of the turf; in later years he owned his own racehorse, adopting the racing colours used by the First Duke of Devonshire.

Cavendish conducted his personal life with greater discretion after he left Cambridge, especially where his amorous adventures were concerned. It soon became clear that his public life would be centred on politics and at the age of twenty-four he entered parliament as Liberal MP for North Lancashire. The fact that he yawned during his maiden speech in the House of Commons typified his disinterested and world-weary manner, though Disraeli commented at the time: 'To anyone who can betray such languor in such circumstances the highest posts should be open'. This was to prove prophetic.

Although Cavendish mainly resided at Devonshire House in Piccadilly and entertained well, he disdained fashion and settled into an indifference to his appearance which he never lost. His clothes were invariably ill-fitting and unsuitable for the occasion and, furthermore, he dropped into crumpled sleep whenever and wherever the languor, or lethargy, or boredom, overcame him.

Yet the keen politician could emerge with surprising determination. In 1858, the year in which he became Lord Hartington upon his father's accession to the Dukedom, he made a move of no confidence which brought about the resignation of Lord Derby's government. The speaker of the House remarked that Hartington possessed 'A power of speaking rarely shown by persons who have had so little practice'.

After a visit to the United States of America at the height of the Civil War, when he met both Abraham Lincoln and Jefferson Davis, Hartington was appointed Under Secretary at the War Office. His hard work in the post led in 1865 to a short period as Secretary of State for War.

IN LOVE FOR LIFE

By this time Lord Hartington had fallen in love, for life, with the Duchess of Manchester, the former Countess Louise von Alten, a society beauty one year younger than himself. Their affair continued in semi-secrecy for the next thirty years, while Louise remained married to the Duke of Manchester. The arrangement was apparently acceptable to the three main parties, in fact Hartington was a regular guest of the Manchesters throughout.

Political acquiescence was a different matter. In April 1868, Hartington supported Gladstone's widely unpopular proposals for the disestablishment of the Irish church although it cost him his seat at the December general election. Within months Hartington obtained a new seat from the Radnor Boroughs. Under Gladstone he served as Postmaster General with a seat in the cabinet and was occupied in nationalising the telegraphs. At the end of 1870 he was appointed Chief Secretary for Ireland.

When Gladstone resigned the Liberal leadership after the party's defeat at the 1874 elections, the position was accorded to Hartington. Two years later the Liberals were returned to power; Queen Victoria asked Hartington to form a government but he bowed to Gladstone's clear suitability for the premiership and deferred in his favour. Hartington was appointed his Secretary of State for India.

In internal affairs Hartington had become recognised leader of the moderate Liberals. After his brother, Lord Frederick Cavendish, was assassinated in Dublin in 1882, Hartington became entirely opposed to Gladstone's views on Home Rule and in May 1886 gave a powerful speech which persuaded a group of dissenting Liberals to ensure the defeat of the Home Rule Bill.

Hartington, now leader of a distinct party, the Liberal Unionists, fought a vigorous campaign at the ensuing general election. The result was a majority for the combined Conservatives and Liberal Unionists. Hartington was offered the premiership but declined in favour of the Conservative leader, Lord Salisbury. Within a matter of months Salisbury was faced with a crisis in his government and offered Hartington yet a third chance to become Prime Minister. This time the matter was resolved before he reached a firm decision.

THE DOUBLE DUCHESS

At the end of 1891 he succeeded to the title of Eighth Duke of Devonshire. The following year, at the age of fifty-nine, he was finally able to marry the recently widowed Louise, to be known in the family as the 'double duchess'. She was the first Duchess of Devonshire for eighty years and immediately began to révitalise both Devonshire House and Chatsworth with lively house parties. The Duchess loved entertaining and, like Harty-Tarty (her pet name for the Duke) was very fond of the card tables. She organised annual Devonshire House Balls, the most magnificent and famous of which was the fancy dress ball held in 1897 to celebrate the Diamond Jubilee of Queen Victoria. The Duke appeared as the Emperor Charles V.

The Prince of Wales, an old friend of both the Duke and Duchess, often dined at Devonshire House - on one occasion his host had to be woken up to welcome him - and regularly joined in pheasant shooting parties at Chatsworth. Later, as King Edward VII, he frequently stayed at Chatsworth with Queen Alexandra. The royal couple particularly enjoyed the New Year house parties where formality was kept to a minimum.

The party-loving Duchess has not quite faded from living memory around Edensor, Baslow, Beeley and Pilsley, where some elderly villagers still remember the wonderful Christmas parties she provided for them as estate children.

Behind the scenes the Duke was taking measures to keep the family debts under control. He sold off estates in Ireland and Derbyshire and property in London, using the capital to invest in stocks and shares.

As far as his political interests were concerned, Devonshire made full use of his seat in the House of Lords. In 1893 Gladstone's second Home Rule bill was thrown out of the Lords following a memorable speech by his old opponent. Two years later Devonshire was appointed Lord President of the Council with responsibility for educational departments and the cabinet defence committee. Under Balfour he became government leader in the House of Lords. In October 1903 he resigned from the cabinet on the issue of tariff reform policy, after which he resigned his chairmanship of the Liberal Unionist Association.

On 7 May 1907, after thirty-four years in the House of Commons and sixteen in the

44

House of Lords, Devonshire gave his final party speech. In mid-June he made his last public appearance when he conferred degrees as Chancellor of Cambridge University. A few days later he was taken ill, having for some time been incapacitated by a heart complaint. At the end of October he and the Duchess left to spend the winter in Egypt but on the way home, on 24 March 1908, the Duke died at Cannes. His last words were: 'Well, the game's over and I'm not sorry'.

Asquith paid him this tribute: '.. in the closing years of his life he commanded in a greater degree than perhaps any other public man the respect and confidence of men of every shade of opinion in this Kingdom', partly, Asquith added, by virtue of his tranquil indifference to praise and blame, and by absolute disinterestedness'.

Three hundred MPs attended the funeral of the Eighth. Duke of Devonshire at Edensor and statues were erected by public subscription in Eastbourne and beside the War Office in London. The Duke's most private papers were destroyed as he had instructed and his Duchess survived him by three years.

The Painted Hall stairs, designed by W.H. Romaine-Walker, 1912.

THE NINTH DUKE OF DEVONSHIRE
(1868-1938)

On the death of the childless Eighth Duke in 1908, the Devonshire title passed to his nephew, Victor Christian William Cavendish, son of Lord Edward Cavendish and the former Lady Emma Lascelles.

He regretfully accepted that the Dukedom would curtail his choice of political direction. At the age of twenty-three Victor Cavendish had been returned as Liberal Unionist MP for West Derbyshire, the youngest member of the House of Commons. He was a most conscientious member of parliament and under Prime Minister Balfour was given the post of Financial Secretary to the Treasury. That administration was defeated in the elections of 1905.

The accession to the title also meant a change of home for the new Duke. Since his marriage in 1892 to Lady Evelyn Fitzmaurice - 'Evie' - elder daughter of the Fifth Marquess of Lansdowne, his home had been Holker Hall in Lancashire. The couple were extremely fond of Holker, where they were bringing up their first six children, and it was a wrench making the move to Chatsworth.

First, though, the great house had to be brought into the 20th century, with major work carried out to the drains and the installation of electricity. Chatsworth became a family home again. Within a few months of moving in, Duchess Evie gave birth to her seventh child, Anne. The Blue Drawing Room was converted into a schoolroom and the staff had a busy core of nannies, governesses and tutors. The Duke was the kindest of fathers and to the end of his life delighted in being surrounded by children.

He entered heartily into local country life, following his favourite interests - cricket (becoming President of Derbyshire Cricket Club), shooting, golf (on his own course) and farming. He was very knowledgeable on agricultural matters, with something of a farmer's heavy build and an unflappable steady nature to match. He introduced Holker shorthorns to Chatsworth and built stables for his Shire horses at Pilsley. In addition he furthered the success of the County Territorial Association and allowed training courses for the Yeomanry and Territorials to take place at Chatsworth.

While the Duke attended to all outdoor affairs, most practical matters concerning the House were left to his wife. She ordered major alterations to the staircase in the Painted Hall and undertook care of the collections; an expert needlewoman, she faultlessly restored the old tapestries herself.

Duchess Evelyn was only a little less imperious than her friend, Queen Mary, to whom she was appointed Mistress of the Robes in 1911. Similarly, Her Grace was also usually spoken of with more respect than affection. Yet she had everyone's interests at heart and was responsible for the establishment of a branch of the Red Cross in Derbyshire.

For many years the family split up the seasons by moving around their other estates. Between November and January they lived at Chatsworth and from February to April at Lismore. Their London house was opened up from May to July. Then they all moved north for grouse shooting at Bolton Abbey, stopping off to visit Bakewell Show en route. The latter part of September saw the family at Hardwick until November came round again.

AT HOME IN OTTOWA

The Ninth Duke's inheritance came burdened with more than half a million pounds owing in death duties. Within a few years he had considerably reduced this by selling various valuable possessions. In addition to lands and Chiswick House, he sold the collection of twenty-five books printed by Caxton in the 15th century and rare volumes of plays purchased by the Sixth Duke.

He maintained his deep interest in politics and regularly took his seat in the House of Lords, acting as Conservative Whip and, in 1915-16, Civil Lord of the Admiralty. His most important and enjoyable role also began in 1916 when he went to Canada as Governor-General and Commander-in-Chief. Duchess Evie and their six youngest children went too - Lord Hartington had been posted to Gallipoli. The family set up home in Ottowa.

The post assigned to the Duke of Devonshire was an important one which he undertook with enthusiasm. He established a good relationship with politicians and also enjoyed a great deal of contact with the Canadian people who 'liked him exceedingly'. During his extensive travels across the country he was able to pursue his interest in agriculture, standing him in good stead for the Presidency of the Royal Agricultural Society, to which he was elected between the wars.

It was in Canada that the family was joined by a young man recovering from war wounds, Harold Macmillan. In 1921 this future British Prime Minister was married to Dorothy, third daughter of the Devonshires.

The family had recently returned to England. On the day that they set sail for home the Duke wrote in his diary: 'V. sad to believe that this is my last day in Canada. Wish the time was beginning again.'

ECONOMIES TO BE MADE

Back in Derbyshire the Devonshires were welcomed at Buxton by Lord Hartington as the town's mayor, before travelling on to Chatsworth. There the war had resulted in major changes. The number of gardeners had been halved to forty and the Great Conservatory had to be demolished. Its upkeep was just too costly and the plants had already suffered from enforced economies in labour and heating.

Devonshire House in Piccadilly, the family's London seat since it was built by the First Duke, was sold in favour of a more practical residence at No. 2 Carlton Gardens, off the Mall. The move reflected the sensible, often parsimonious influence of Duchess Evie.

The next few years were busy ones for the Duke. When the Conservatives came to power in 1922 he was brought into the cabinet as Bonar Law's Secretary of the Colonies. The job gave him immense satisfaction and he spent his weekdays in Westminster, always well-informed and dealing conscientiously with major issues, notably problems in Kenya arising from demands for settlement rights from Asian immigrants, as citizens of the British Empire.

The Duke's speech on the matter became known in part as the Devonshire Declaration, the basis for support from future British Governments for independence throughout Black Africa. In a Government White Paper, Devonshire wrote: '.. the interests of the African natives must be paramount' with administration centred on 'the protection and advancement of the native races.'

Amongst his non-political responsibilities the Duke in 1923 became High Steward of Cambridge University, where as an undergraduate he had been President of the Amateur Dramatic Club. In 1924 he was greatly honoured to be put in charge of preparations for the British Empire Exhibition at Wembley. He was conscientious and tireless in his efforts but the work probably put a strain on his health.

The following Easter, 1925, whilst on holiday at Lismore with his family, the Duke suffered a stroke. Although he recovered physically, his personality was sadly changed. No longer good-humoured and gentlemanly, he became irascible, short-tempered and rude to everyone around him. The Duchess had to become even more the efficient organiser. This was very noticeable at Chatsworth, where her tight hold on expenditure left the staff balancing loyalty against shortage of jobs. Her Grace kept an eagle eye on all outgoings, even down to the meals eaten 'below stairs'.

A small admission charge was introduced at Chatsworth, but only to raise funds for local hospitals. In the 1930s the cost was one shilling for an adult, sixpence per child. In 1926 the Chatsworth Estates Company had been formed, the first move towards limiting further death duties. Under the law it was vital for the Ninth Duke to live at least a further three years, and he did. Throughout his sixties he continued to enjoy the outdoor life, attending cricket matches, supervising his beloved Shire horses and shooting on the estate. Winter shooting parties were held at Chatsworth every Christmas. In 1933 George V and Queen Mary stayed with the Devonshires when they paid a visit to the Royal Show at Derby.

But gradually the Duke became more reclusive, in pain from gout and with patience for none but his smallest grandchildren, who adored him in turn. Public appearances grew increasingly rare and on 6 May 1938, the Ninth Duke of Devonshire died at Chatsworth House, survived by Evie, their two sons and five daughters.

Churchdale Hall.

THE TENTH DUKE OF DEVONSHIRE
(1895-1950)

As far as the family finances were concerned, Edward William Spencer Cavendish broke the mould. His inheritance would not come lumbered with massive debts and, unlike certain of his predecessors, extravagance was not in his nature.

As Lord Hartington he was married in 1917 to Lady Mary Cecil, second daughter of the Marquis of Salisbury. In the early years of their marriage the couple lived at Hardwick Hall but later moved into Churchdale Hall at Ashford-in-the-Water with their young family: William, Andrew, Elizabeth and Anne.

In 1923, the year that his father the Ninth Duke bowed out of political life, 'Eddie' Hartington was returned as Conservative MP for West Derbyshire. A deep interest in politics may have been a family tradition but his own course was undertaken completely from choice. From 1936-1940 he held the post of Parliamentary Under-Secretary for the Dominions, taking him on extensive visits to Australia and South Africa. He remained in Chamberlain's government when he acceded to the Dukedom in 1938.

With the death of the Ninth Duke, the Dowager Duchess moved into Hardwick Hall, leaving Chatsworth for its rather reluctant new occupants, her son and his family. They did not want to leave the more homely Churchdale and had recent memories of rather formal dinner parties at Chatsworth with the Ninth Duke, not the most genial of hosts after his stroke.

However, Chatsworth was the ducal seat and the new Duchess began to plan changes to make everyday life more comfortable. A passenger lift was to be installed and an electric 'railway' was designed to bring dishes to the dining room from the distant kitchens. Meanwhile, the Duke made himself at home in down-to-earth style. He was a skilled handyman and is remembered for practising carpentry in the dining room. In August 1939, over three thousand guests attended a series of parties held at Chatsworth to celebrate the coming of age and accession to the title of Lord Hartington, of the heir, William Cavendish.

A DIRECT HIT

Within weeks the country was at war with Germany. The Devonshires suspended their plans for alterations at Chatsworth and moved back to Churchdale Hall. Pre-empting moves to have the family seat taken over for military use, the Duke leased Chatsworth House to Penrhos College, a girls' boarding school. The contents of the house were packed and crated in only eleven days and silk-covered and panelled walls were carefully boarded over. Three hundred pupils and their staff moved in.

The Chatsworth servants dispersed, some into 'useful work' such as agriculture and others into the Forces. Lord Hartington and Lord Andrew Cavendish joined the Coldstream Guards. They both saw active service leading up to Allied victories as events took their course in Europe.

The new occupants of Chatsworth were allowed complete freedom of the house, gardens, parks and woods. Only the library was excluded from general use - here were stacked precious pictures and pieces of furniture. The Painted Hall was used as a chapel and assembly hall and for film shows. The large dining room became a dormitory -- so cold that the girls slept in their dressing gowns - and the theatre was used for dramatic productions, parties and dances. In the summer the girls swam in one of the upper lakes and in winter they skated on the Canal Pond at the side of the house. When Sheffield suffered air-raids the beer cellars of Chatsworth became air-raid shelters. According to one resident pupil of the time, two enemy aircraft machine-gunned the house one night, presumably because it was a possible military establishment. In her book *The House*, the present Duchess of Devonshire mentions only that a stray bullet from an American aircraft, on an exercise over the moors, scored a direct hit on a table in the library.

During the War the Duke of Devonshire remained a minister in the Government of Winston Churchill and in 1942 was Appointed Under-Secretary of State for India and

Burma, having earlier turned down Churchill's offer of the Viceroyalty of India.

Whilst at Westminster he usually returned to Compton Place in Eastbourne at weekends, an easier journey than returning to the Peak. His London house in Carlton Gardens was damaged by German incendiaries.

POLITICAL DEFEAT

The two sons of the Duke and Duchess of Devonshire were married during the war. In April 1941, Lord Andrew married Deborah Freeman-Mitford, daughter of the Second Baron Redesdale. Three years later 'Billy' Hartington married Kathleen Kennedy, daughter of the American Ambassador to London (and sister to a future President of the United States of America). She worked for the British Red Cross in England.

Shortly before his marriage, Lord Hartington had suffered a political defeat which was seen as a sign of the changing times. In line with family tradition he had been offered, and accepted, the Conservative nomination for west Derbyshire in a by-election. He was granted leave to fight his opponent, Independent Socialist Charles White.

'Charlie' White spoke out against what he saw as the virtual entitlement of the upper-classes to a political role. He took a stand for an end to this 'birthright'. Lord Hartington could not justify the old social order but positioned himself instead as a tester for the popularity of Churchill's government. The results were declared at Matock Town Hall, giving Alderman White a majority of 4,561.

Lord Hartington rejoined his unit and in May he was married to Kathleen Kennedy. Five weeks later his battalion was sent to France and on 9 September he was killed by a German sniper in Belgium. In 1948 the widowed Marchioness of Hartington died in an air crash; she is buried at Edensor.

CHATSWORTH RE-OPENED

The tragic death of Lord Hartington had a profound effect on his father. Whilst still in mourning he was presented with the additional worry of protecting the family wealth in the face of new government legislation on death duties. In 1946 the Duke updated the Chatsworth Estates Company, establishing the Chatsworth Settlement Trust to which his shares were transferred. It merely remained for him to live a further three years. Even though the period was extended to five years in the 1946 budget, the Duke was still only fifty-one and there was no need to worry on account of his state of health. In 1948 the maximum rate of death duties was increased to 80%.

Meanwhile, Chatsworth had been empty since Penrhos College left in 1946. The house was in dire need of redecoration but only £150 worth of painting was permissible under existing restrictions. The Duke and Duchess were more than pleased to continue using

52

their homes at Ashford, Eastbourne and London.

During 1948, preparations began to re-open Chatsworth the following year. Over the Easter period of 1949, 75,000 visitors arrived, paying half-a-crown (22 1/2p) admittance to the house and a shilling (5p) to see the gardens.

As the 1940s drew to a close, the Duke of Devonshire could look ahead to the spring of 1951 and an end to the threat of death duties. But in November 1950, just over three months before the expiry of the 'quarantine' period which it had been so essential for him to survive, he died suddenly at his Eastbourne home. The fifty-five year old Duke had suffered a fatal heart attack while enjoying his 'favourite occupation' of chopping wood.

A massive 80% death duties was levied on the Devonshire estate. The figure owed to the Treasury was £4.72 million. Unless paid immediately the interest amounted to £1,000 per day. Andrew Robert Buxton Cavendish, Eleventh Duke of Devonshire, had acceded to a title hamstrung with what seemed like an insurmountable debt.

The Hunting Tower, taken in the year of 'Devonshire 300'.

THE ELEVENTH DUKE OF DEVONSHIRE

A Cavendish has held the Devonshire title, first as Earl and subsequently as Duke, for fourteen generations. In 1994 the Eleventh Duke of Devonshire took the dukedom into its tercentenary.

Speaking at Chatsworth in the early weeks of 1995 the Duke, informally known as Andrew, reminisced over his life to date. Although a tentative start has been made on his autobiography, it is not, he mused, 'too likely to see the light of day'. Perhaps the reason partly lies in the words of Brian Masters in his book *The Dukes* 'A Cavendish is ... studious, calm, cool, unflustered. On the whole, however, their intelligence does not publicise itself because a Cavendish does not have much energy. He likes to be left in peace.'

After listening carefully as the extract was read to him, Andrew agreed that it was in fact 'absolutely accurate'. Yet events have shown that he possesses reserves of determination to carry him through exceptionally testing times.

Second son of the Tenth Duke of Devonshire, Lord Andrew Robert Buxton Cavendish was born on 2 January 1920 at 20 Arlington Street, London W1, the home of his maternal grandfather and now part of the Ritz. He was educated at Eton and Trinity College, Cambridge. By the time that fate placed him in the line of succession he was a young married man. His elder brother, William Lord Hartington and heir to the dukedom, died in action in 1944 and there were no children from his marriage to Kathleen Kennedy.

Naturally, it had been William who had grown up with his future more or less mapped out. Andrew had hoped to be free to pursue a career in publishing after the war, once describing this interest as 'a nice mix of judgement and gambling'.

In April 1941 he had married Deborah Vivian Freeman-Mitford, youngest daughter of the Second Baron Redesdale. The wedding took place at the church of St Bartholomew the Great in Smithfield. As Lieutenant Lord Andrew Cavendish, the groom was serving with the Coldstream Guards and in the early part of their marriage the couple travelled together wherever he was posted. After the birth of their first daughter, Emma, in 1943, Deborah stayed behind and made their family home at 'The Rookery' at Ashford in the Water. In August 1944 Andrew, now a captain, took part in action in Italy during which he won the M.C. for gallantry in battle. He rose to the rank of major, albeit briefly, before leaving the army.

His son and heir, Peregrine - nicknamed 'Sto' - was born in 1944 and a second daughter, Sophie, in 1957.

In the intervening years Lord Andrew had twice attempted to secure a seat in parliament, standing as Conservative candidate for the Labour stronghold of Chesterfield in the general elections of 1945 and 1950. On both occasions he was disappointed, beaten by 13,000 and 17,000 votes respectively.

SAVING CHATSWORTH

Within months of the second defeat all outside interests suddenly had to be put to one side. In November, while on business in Australia, he received news of the unexpected death of his father at the early age of fifty-five. The blow of close bereavement came with the knowledge that overnight he had inherited a dukedom burdened with a pressing debt of almost £5 million in death duties.

Andrew reflects that two factors were to save the day. Firstly, he was young. Secondly, he had what he describes as wonderful legal and financial advisers. 'If they had panicked,' he says with conviction, 'all would have been lost.' This modest statement,

55

however, does not tell the full story. More is revealed in the words of a very close observer, the Duchess of Devonshire in her book *The House - A Portrait of Chatsworth:* 'Although he' (Andrew) 'had advice from many people, it washe and he alone who had to decide the best way of raising the millions of pounds which the law demanded. The responsibility for this decision was a heavy one and he was preoccupied by it for years. He pondered and considered the means by which the money could be raised which would have the least bad effect on the collections, the estate and succeeding generations of his family. Chatsworth was always at the centre of his thoughts and his plans'.

Attempts to reduce the debt by legal action failed. Total valuation of Cavendish assets was agreed with the Inland Revenue at £5.9 million and it became obvious that possessions would have to be disposed of; interest was accumulating at £1,000 per day. Sentiment backed up the decision that all efforts should be made to keep Chatsworth intact. This would clearly have to be at the expense of other properties and first to be sold were lands in Derbyshire and an agricultural estate in Scotland. In the Peak the loss of property was considerable, notably in Buxton and Peak Forest. Still intact within the estate are Edensor, Pilsley, a large part of Beeley and significant holdings at Baslow.

A poignant sacrifice was made in 1959 when, several years after the idea was first proposed by Andrew, the government accepted Hardwick Hall as another instalment against the remaining debt. The property has always been close to Cavendish hearts, having been built and occupied by Bess of Hardwick, mother of the First Earl of Devonshire. Hardwick, its contents and parkland were transferred by the government to the National Trust. In a separate deal the Treasury had already agreed to accept possessions valued at more than £1,200,000 in lieu of duties. This entailed the sale of ten major works of art from the Chatsworth collections.

Not until 17 May 1967 was the last pound of duty paid. It still remained for a deficit to be cleared on the Trustees' income account, from which estate income had been borrowed to meet interest payments on the debt. This settlement took a further seven years.

By this time, total Cavendish acreage had been reduced by a third and management of the Derbyshire estates was now centralised at Chatsworth, to be run as a business with a necessary eye to profit. Today the trustees of the Chatsworth Settlement own 35,000 acres in Derbyshire - containing 450 dwellings - and 30,000 acres at Bolton Abbey in North Yorkshire. Lismore Castle and 8,000 acres in Waterford, inherited by Andrew in 1944 upon the death of his uncle, Lord Charles Cavendish, are held by the Lismore Trust within the Chatsworth Settlement. Andrew owns only a house in London in his own right.

A STATELY HOME

In the late 1950s an important change came about at Chatsworth House. Since 1947 Andrew and his family had lived at Edensor House but about ten years later the decision was made, not without some reservations, to move into Chatsworth. Its future was to be as a stately home open to the public and it was correctly predicted that a resident ducal family would draw visitors. In any case, the days of countless low-paid servants were over and it was impossible for the great mansion of 175 rooms and 17 staircases to become a home in its entirety. Preparations for the move took a year and a half, largely carried out by the treasured and immensely enthusiastic staff. The family moved into their newly prepared private quarters in the autumn of 1959.

Even after clearing the great debt it became necessary to sell further works of art to offset the losses of running Chatsworth. Then in 1975, the introduction of Capital Transfer Tax eroded the advantages of the existing trust settlement and radical administrative measures had to be planned. Therefore a unique, independent charitable trust was set up, with the approval of the Treasury, 'for the long term preservation of Chatsworth and its essential contents for the public benefit.'

In 1981 upon establishment of this, the Chatsworth House Trust, the Duke of Devonshire became a sub-tenant of the House, paying a full market rent for his family's accommodation.

In April of that year a painting from the Chatsworth collection, Poussin's Holy Family, realised £1,650,000 at auction. The sale of rare books followed and the total proceeds went into endowing the Trust to enable the House to stay open to the public. In July 1984 the Trust benefited from a sale of seventy-one Old Master drawings which realised £21 million at Christie's, then a world record auction figure and three times the expected sum.

Maintenance costs for the House and Estate depend on income from the Trust in addition to visitors' entrance fees and special events. All such revenue is vital but nothing is allowed to spoil the special country atmosphere of Chatsworth. Annual Angling and Country Fairs are firmly established whilst local organisations benefit in turn from such events as coffee mornings held in the Painted Hall. The House itself is now open to visitors on more days than ever before.

Private visitors regularly include members of the royal family and prominent guests from overseas. The late Rose Kennedy, mother to Kathleen Marchioness of Hartington, was a particularly welcome guest well into her eighties. Her son, John F. Kennedy, stayed here when he visited the grave of his sister Kathleen at Edensor. The Duke was present at both his Presidential inauguration and his funeral. Senator Edward Kennedy maintains the link between the two families as an occasional guest of the Devonshires.

GARDENING AND COMMERCE

From their earliest times here, the Duke and Duchess have enjoyed planning improvements to the gardens together. One early venture was the planting of a serpentine beech hedge to enclose the bust, on its marble pillar, of the Bachelor Duke. In 1962 a yew maze, designed by Comptroller Dennis Fisher, was planted on the former site of Paxton's Great Conservatory. An uncompromisingly 20th-century conservatory was erected in 1970; it contains three controlled climates - tropical, Mediterranean and temperate - and produces exotic fruits.

To mark the 1994 tercentenary celebrations, an avenue of limes is to be grown between the Golden Gates and the House. The Prince of Wales has planted a tree, as has Senator Edward Kennedy in memory of his sister and brother-in-law. The planting of memorial trees is already an established tradition at Chatsworth and permission is generally freely given. Some trees commemorate departed friends and relatives who enjoyed happy times here, others have been planted by appreciative visitors themselves.

As for the House, Andrew made an early decision to replace the plate glass windows of the south front with small bevelled panes for a more pleasing effect, though all choice of interior design and re-arrangements have been left to Deborah with his blessing. To anyone who reads her book on the House it is clear that this has been a labour of love and her personal involvement has been total. She also has a free hand in farming matters, having become a top breeder and judge of certain breeds of poultry, cattle and ponies, notably Haflingers.

Deborah confesses to a 'passion for commerce' and has established a shop in the Orangery, a restaurant in the former Carriage House and a farm shop at Pilsley. This latter utilises the old Shire Horse stud complex, of which the remaining buildings have been converted and let to various artists and craftspeople.

Meanwhile Chatsworth House has once more become a collector's showplace. Pursuing his own preferences, Andrew has added considerably to the library as well as purchasing and commissioning works from living artists. Additions include family portraits by Lucien Freud, sculptures by Angela Conner, and Samuel Palmer water colours. The mineral collection started by Georgiana, wife of the Fifth Duke, has also been expanded.

PARK TOP

In an interview with Sue Macgregor for the radio programme Conversation Piece in 1980, Andrew revealed that he only bought works of art when revenue from racing allowed, in fact he had a system of combining his art and racing accounts. By this means he acquired works including a 'marvellous Lowry' from the winnings of his mare, Park Top.

Racing is one of his lifelong loves. He bought his first racehorse in 1948 and adopted the pale yellow silks - properly described as 'straw' - used by the First Duke of Devonshire. The First Duke chose these colours when this form of identification was first introduced; they are the oldest registered colours still in use.

To date Park Top has been Andrew's only truly successful racehorse. Purchased for a modest 500 guineas and trained by Bernard van Cutsem, she raced between 1967 and 1970 and her earnings made her the second highest stakes-winning mare in European racing history. Amongst her fourteen victories were the Ribblesdale Stakes at Royal Ascot, the Coronation Cup, The Hardwicke Stakes and the King George VI & Queen Elizabeth Stakes.

Lester Piggott described Park Top as 'The best of her sex I've ever ridden' and in 1970 she was voted Flat Race-horse of the Year. Pieces of jewellery and a sculpture were commissioned in her likeness but her owner's personal tribute is his own book: *Park Top, a Romance of the Turf.*

This emotive excerpt from the book, reproduced by kind permission of the author, refers to the mare's last race at Longchamp in October 1970. Her defeat brought bitter regrets that she had not been retired after her last great win. It was also the memorable day when her owner, very publicly, lost his customary sang-froid:

'I have said of racing that the tears come when one wins and not when one loses. That October day in the Bois de Boulogne came near to being the exception. As we waited for her to return to be unsaddled I was close to tears, not tears of disappointment but tears of anguish for having let the defeat happen. Luckily, the unbelievable behaviour of the French crowd saved the day. As Park Top was led in, the Longchamp race-goers began to boo ... I could not believe my ears. For that crowd to boo Park Top, the mare they had taken to their hearts and from whom she had received as much, if not more, adulation than from race-goers in England, was like hearing a great prima donna being booed for faltering over one note. My anguish gave way to fury and, turning to face the crowd, I repeatedly gave them that two-fingered gesture later made famous by Harvey Smith in a much publicised incident at Hickstead. I have always been slightly jealous of him for getting the credit for bringing this singularly expressive gesture into the public eye. I feel the credit should go to me.'

A painting of Park Top, with Piggott in the saddle, occupies an eye-level position at the centre of Andrew's desk. He still keeps a handful of racehorses but knows that 'There will never be another Park Top', then he adds, '...and I think I'm rather pleased'.

MOVING WITH THE TIMES

Andrew also inherited the traditional Devonshire interest in politics but other demands on his time have denied him a more active political life. He originally took his seat in the House of Lords as a Conservative and in 1956 gave his maiden speech on the subject of Suez - a brave choice, he feels, at a time when that name was inseparable from the word 'crisis'. Under Macmillan and, subsequently, Douglas-Home, he served as Parliamentary Under-Secretary of State for Commonwealth Relations from 1960 to 1962, then as Minister of State in the Commonwealth Relations Office until 1964. He also acted as Minister for Colonial Affairs between 1963 and 1964. Since that time he has held no political office, though his views received a public airing in 1982 when he joined the Social Democrats as a staunch 'David Owen man'.

Today the Duke sits on the cross-benches of the House, describing himself as a *'middle woodsman'* and pleased to be *'unwhippable'*. Whilst he now spends most of his time at Chatsworth he always attends debates in which he has an interest - most recently one concerning forestry.

Outside of politics, Andrew has held a wide variety of positions. Locally these have included serving as Mayor of Buxton (1952-54) Vice-Lieutenant of Derbyshire (1957-87) and a long period as President of the Sheffield Branch of the Coldstream Association. He continues as National Vice-President of the Coldstream Association but otherwise his one remaining role is the Presidency of the National Society for Deaf Children, from which he will retire when a successor is found.

FAMILY AND COMMUNITY

As for the succession to the dukedom, this is assured for the foreseeable future. In 1967 Peregrine Lord Hartington married Amanda Heywood-Lonsdale and their first child, William Lord Burlington, was born in 1969. The Duke and Duchess now have eight grandchildren and one great-grandchild.

The estate community which centres on the Devonshires consists of some 750 people, of whom about 150 are deeply appreciated working staff. Staff care is wide-ranging, from the provision of social facilities to good family housing and a guaranteed estate home for life on retirement.

In May 1994 the Chatsworth community and large numbers of local people shared in one of the highlights of recent years - the 300th anniversary of the creation of the Devonshire Dukedom. Over 3,000 guests shared in the celebrations. A local actor, Richard Evans, was commissioned to write a masque Performance, presented after a Supper Party in the grounds beside the river.

Local children were in the cast and the evening ended with a firework spectacular. In total, over £46,000 was raised for the Children's Society as a result of 'Devonshire 300' events.

The 1994 Flower Festival also exceeded all expectations. It is held only every ten years and on this occasion filled a record number of marquees. Andrew recalls with clear delight the spectacular success of both the Flower Festival and the coffee morning which attracted a massive response of 6,000 visitors in support of Ashgate Hospice. The year also saw the transmission of a behind-the-scenes television series on Chatsworth which brought an apparent increase in visitors, though to some extent this was offset by competition from the newer diversions of Carsington Water. By and large, there are advantages to moving with the times at Chatsworth - the recent relaxation on Sunday trading laws was promptly applied to the farm shop.

So much for the past and the present but Chatsworth also has to look ahead. Thoughts are already beginning to turn towards millennium celebrations, which will coincide with Andrew's golden jubilee as Duke of Devonshire and his own 80th birthday. Not that he takes anything for granted. After very patiently reviewing his life to date, he shared this confidence: 'I remind myself every morning and every evening that I am one of the luckiest people in the world.' And the emphasis, he stressed, is on the word 'remind'.

History will return the compliment, reminding future generations how lucky it was for Chatsworth to have had the Eleventh Duke of Devonshire at its seat.

BIBLIOGRAPHY

The House, A Portrait of Chatsworth The Duchess of Devonshire (Macmillan 1982)
Stags & Serpents John Pearson (Macmillan 1983)
The Dukes Brian Masters (Blond & Briggs 1980)
Park Top, A Romance of the Turf Andrew Devonshire (London Magazine 1976)

The Cavendish family tree.

1505 - 1557 Sir William Cavendish = Bess of Hardwick c1527 - 1608

1552 - 1625 William Cavendish = Anne Keighley - 1625
1st Earl of Devonshire (1618)

1590 - 1628 William Cavendish = Hon. Christian Bruce 1595 - 1675
2nd Earl of Devonshire.

1617 -1684 William Cavendish = Lady Elizabeth Cecil 1619 - 1689
3rd Earl of Devonshire

1640 - 1707 William Cavendish = Lady Mary Butler 1646 - 1710
4th Earl of Devonshire
1st Duke of Devonshire 1694

1673 - 1729 William Cavendish = Hon. Rachel Russell 1674 - 1725
2nd Duke of Devonshire

1698 - 1755 William Cavendish = Catherine Hoskins - 1777
3rd Duke of Devonshire

1720 - 1764 William Cavendish = Lady Charlotte Boyle 1731 - 1754
4th Duke of Devonshire

1748 - 1811 William Cavendish = (1) Lady Georgiana Spencer 1757 - 1806
5th Duke of Devonshire = (2) Lady Elizabeth Foster 1759 - 1824

1754 - 1834 George Cavendish = Lady Elizabeth Compton 1760 - 1835

1783 - 1812 William Cavendish = Hon. Louisa O'Callaghan - 1863

1790 - 1858 William Spencer Cavendish   Lady Georgiana Cavendish
6th Duke of Devonshire   = George Howard 1773 - 1848

1803 -1881 Lady Caroline Howard = Hon. William Lascelles 1798 - 1851

1812 -1840 Lady Blanche Howard = William Cavendish 1808 -1891
7th Duke of Devonshire

1833 -1908 Spencer Compton Cavendish = Louise von Alten 1832 -1911
8th Duke of Devonshire.

1838 - 1920 Emma Lascelles = Lord Edward Cavendish 1838 - 1891

1868 - 1938 Victor Cavendish = Lady Evelyn Fitzmaurice 1870 - 1960
9th Duke of Devonshire

1895 - 1950 Edward Cavendish = Lady Mary Cecil 1895 - 1988
10th Duke of Devonshire

1920 - Andrew Cavendish = Hon. Deborah Mitford 1920 -
11th Duke of Devonshire

1944 - Peregrine Cavendish = Amanda Heywood Lonsdale 1944 -
Marquess of Hartington

1969 - William Cavendish - Earl of Burlington

Derbyshire Heritage Series -

ANGLO-SAXON & VIKING DERBYSHIRE by *Richard Bunting.*
ARTISTS WITH DERBYSHIRE CONNECTIONS by *Harold Fearnehough*
BUXTON WATERS - A history of Buxton by *M.Langham & C. Wells*
THE CAPTIVE QUEEN IN DERBYSHIRE - Mary Queen of Scots - by *E.Eisenberg*
CASTLE & MANORS IN AND AROUND DERBYSHIRE by *Mike Smith*
CELTIC DERBYSHIRE by *Peter J. Naylor*
CHURCHES OF DERBYSHIRE by *John J. Anderson* .
DERBY CHINA THROUGH THREE CENTURIES by *Myra Challand*
DERBY CITY STREET TO STREET GUIDE
DERBYSHIRE CHARACTERS FOR YOUNG PEOPLE by *E. Eisenberg*
DERBYSHIRE CHURCHYARDS by *Joyce Critchlow* .
DERBYSHIRE'S MONASTIC HERITAGE by *Michael Smith*
DERBYSHIRE NOTEBOOK - *illustrated by E. Kazimierczuk*
DERBYSHIRE SUPERLATIVES by *Julie Bunting*
THE DERBYSHIRE YEAR - Customs through the years - by *E. Eisenberg*
EYAM, THE PLAGUE AND AN 1858 RAMBLE by *Clarence Daniel*
FLORENCE NIGHTINGALE by *Norma Keen*
FROM THE CRADLE TO THE GRAVE by *E. Eisenberg*
GAZETTER OF THE WHITE PEAK by *Les Robson*
GRANDFATHER THOMAS JACKSON'S RECIPES by *Thomas Jackson*
MANORS & FAMILIES OF DERBYSHIRE *Vol 1 (A - L)*
MANORS & FAMILIES OF DERBYSHIRE *Vol 2 (M - Z)*
MAY THE LORD HAVE MERCY ON YOUR SOUL by *Phillip Taylor*
NOTABLE DERBYSHIRE FAMILIES - family history - by *Roy Christian*
THE OWNERS OF MELBOURNE HALL by *Howard Usher*
THE PEAKLAND ABeCeDARY by *Jule Bunting*
PEAKLAND CHRONOLOGY by *Julie Bunting*
PREHISTORIC DERBYSHIRE by *Gerda & John Pickin*
RIVERS OF DERBYSHIRE by *Harold Fearnehough*
ROMAN DERBYSHIRE by *John Anderson*
STUART DERBYSHIRE by *Joy Childs*
SWARKESTONE BRIDGE & THE STANTON CAUSEWAY by *G.R. Heath*
THIS COSTLY COUNTESS - Bess of Hardwick - by *E. Eisenberg*
TUDOR DERBYSHIRE by *Joy Childs*
WALK THROUGH DERBY - *facsimile first published in 1827*

THE WATER CURE by *Alan Bower*

WOMEN OF DERBYSHIRE by *Susan Watson*

WORK & PLAY - Derbyshire, a photographic record - *by Alan Bower*

WRITERS WITH DERBYSHIRE CONNECTIONS by *Jane Darrall*

SPAGHETTI & BARBED WIRE - True World War 11 escapes story -
by Jack E. Fox

DERBYSHIRE GRAVES - 100 true and unusual graves - *by Peter Naylor*

ON THIS DAY....IN DERBYSHIRE - events that happened throughout the
year - *by John E. Heath*

THE EARLS AND DUKES OF DEVONSHIRE by *Julie Bunting*

TIMMY GLASS WAISTCOAT - Early 20th century life in Clay Cross
recalled - *by Jack E. Fox*

COAL, CHOCOLATE & CHIPS - 1940's and 50's life in Ripley -
by Aileen Watson.

JOHN SMEDLEY of Matlock *by John Large.*

STORIES OF THE DERBYSHIRE DALES *by John Large*

JOSEPH PAXTON *by John Large*

DERBYSHIRE STAINED GLASS WINDOWS - *by Dr. Joyce Critchlow*

LOST VILLAGES OF DERBYSHIRE - *by Peter Naylor*

CROMFORD - A HISTORY - *by Peter Naylor*

THE WEAVERS KNOT - life in the mills of North Derbyshire fictionalised
by Rosie Fellows

ELERGY OF AN EDWARDIAN CHILDHOOD IN DERBYSHIRE - Glossop
area - *by Ian Harlow*

SPIT, POLISH AND BULL - life in Clay Cross continued - *by Jack E. Fox*

A PEAKLAND WILDLIFE YEAR by *Richard Bunting*

COUNTRY POETRY by *Leslie Williamson*

NORMAN & MEDIEVAL DERBYSHIRE by *Richard Bunting*

THE CIVIL WAR IN THE TRENT VALLEY by *Andrew Polkey*